Peace Pipe

Dreams

Peace Pipe

The TRUTH about

DARRELL

Dreams

LIES *about* INDIANS

DENNIS

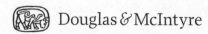 Douglas & McIntyre

Dedicated to the memory of Ken Dennis: father, activist and self-proclaimed "King of the Shuswaps."

DOUGLAS AND MCINTYRE (2013) LTD.

P.O. Box 219, Madeira Park, BC, VON 2H0

www.douglas-mcintyre.com

Edited by Silas White

Indexed by Nicola Goshulak

Text design by Shed Simas

Cover design by Shed Simas and Anna Comfort O'Keeffe

Printed and bound in Canada

 Canada Council Conseil des Arts
for the Arts du Canada

 BRITISH COLUMBIA
ARTS COUNCIL
An agency of the Province of British Columbia

Douglas and McIntyre (2013) Ltd. acknowledges financial support from the Government of Canada through the Canada Book Fund and the Canada Council for the Arts, and from the Province of British Columbia through the BC Arts Council and the Book Publishing Tax Credit.

Cataloguing information available from Library and Archives Canada

ISBN 978-1-77100-040-6 (paper)   **ISBN** 978-1-77100-362-9 (ebook)

Contents

7 NATIVE NAMES
"What do we call you this week?"

30 NATIVE PERCEPTIONS: THE EUROPEAN P.O.V.
"Walk like an In-di-an"

46 NATIVE PERCEPTIONS: THE NORTH AMERICAN P.O.V.
"Our home and Native land?"

84 NATIVES & ALCOHOL
"Why the only Indian on *Cheers* was a wooden Indian"

110 RELIGION & RESIDENTIAL SCHOOLS
"Peace pipe dreams"

137 TREATIES
"Sign on the dotted lie"

165 NATIVE LAND
"Let's call ahead and make reservations"

198 NATIVE GOVERNMENT
"Chief and council or flotsam and jetsam?"

227 THE FUTURE
"Indianfinity and beyond!"

230 A NOTE ON SOURCES

233 INDEX

NATIVE NAMES

"What do we call you this week?"

WHEN I WAS A MUCH YOUNGER MAN AND POSSESSED a much slimmer waistline, I worked for a stint as a desk manager in a New York City health club. I mention my occupation and location for two reasons:

1) to wistfully remind myself that I was once fit enough to work in a health club; and

2) to point out that New York is generally considered a hotbed of intellectual sophistication.

With that in mind, one day I was chatting with a co-worker — a typical, educated New Yorker — when she finally mustered the courage to pop the question that had been nagging her ever since she discovered I was "Native American" and not Puerto Rican. "Why are there so many American Indians in Canada?" she asked. "Was there a lot of immigration back in the day?"

When I finally stopped laughing, I realized her question may not be so ridiculous after all. As an educated New Yorker she was probably taught in school that America's first inhabitants were called "Indian" but now prefer "American Indian" or "Native American"—emphasis on the word *American*. It probably never occurred to her that the first inhabitants were spread across the continent long before borders were drawn. As an educated New Yorker, she was probably too busy contemplating apartment prices and square footage to ponder a people that make up less than two percent of the US population.

8

When I moved back to Canada, I discovered the confusion over what to call this continent's first inhabitants was not limited to the insularity of our southern neighbours. Over the years I have been approached by numerous Canadians who have demanded I provide them with an all-encompassing politically correct word to ensure that they do not offend me, my people or my ancestors. To paraphrase J.R.R. Tolkien, "One word to rule them all and in political correctness bind them."

I am fully sympathetic to their plight. Nothing is more painful to watch than non-Natives attempting to relay a story they saw on the news about some "Native... um... First Nations... er... Aboriginal... uh... Person of Pigment..." and by the time they have gone through the entire list of PC names they usually forget what they were talking about and just end up going home. Personally, I prefer to be called "Supreme Ruler of the Universe," but since no one has jumped on the chance to refer to me as such, I usually provide my stock answer when pressed about terminology for my people: *"First Nations" is the popular term in Canada, "Native American" or "American Indian" in the US, and you should stay away from plain old "Indian" in both countries.*

It's a pat answer and I'm sure that as people read this I will be bombarded with reasons why none of the terms are correct. The problem is there are so many words bandied about to describe my racial situation that it's impossible to provide a term that all Native people can be comfortable with. For example, the word "Indian" is used amongst fellow "Indians" but there will always be "Indians" who are offended by the word "Indian" even though they support their fellow "Indians" using the word "Indian." It's generally considered bad form to call an "Indian" an "Indian" if you yourself are not an "Indian," and that includes "Indians" from India. Got it?

Even my frequent use of the word "Native" has been pounced on from time to time, especially by armchair etymologists who love to question the word usage of poor souls still shackled to the indoctrination of political correctness. These people can usually be found in their natural habitat: the comments section on every web page everywhere. This form of douchebaggery can also be found while crossing the US–Canadian border. The following is a short skit that illustrates numerous conversations I have had with border guards over my self-identification. For tonight's performance, the part of DARRELL will be played by me.

FADE IN

INT. AIRPORT CUSTOMS — EVERY TIME

A tired and jet-lagged DARRELL (ME) approaches a CUSTOMS OFFICER. Darrell is immediately "randomly selected."

CUSTOMS OFFICER: Citizenship?

DARRELL: I'm Native.

CUSTOMS OFFICER: We're all native to somewhere. Where are you native to?

DARRELL: I'm Native to this continent.

CUSTOMS OFFICER: I was born here, that means I'm native to this continent too. What are you?

DARRELL: I'm Native American.

CUSTOMS OFFICER: What state are you from?

DARRELL: No, I'm Native American from Canada.

CUSTOMS OFFICER: So you're an Eskimo.

DARRELL: The word is Inuit, and no, I'm from Canada, that makes me First Nations.

CUSTOMS OFFICER: What's that, like, the United Nations?

DARRELL: NO, I'M AN INDIAN!

DARRELL places two fingers behind his head to represent feathers and dances around in a circle.

DARRELL: Woo Woo Woo Woo!! Hey ya ya ya. Hey ya ya ya.

CUSTOMS OFFICER: Oh, why didn't you say so? Welcome to North Dakota.

FADE OUT.

I know what you're thinking: "Why don't you just say 'American' or 'Canadian'? Why do you have to be such a pain in the ass?" And therein lies the complicated nature of Native self-identification. Allow me to illuminate.

I am a Status Indian, which means I am registered with an Indian reserve in Canada and therefore eligible for certain rights not afforded "Canadians" or "Americans" (a.k.a. "regular folk"). As a Status Indian I am allowed free passage between the US and Canada due to a little piece of legislation from 1794 called the Jay Treaty. Back then, Native people were an important political and military force in North America, so certain concessions were made to us. Indians, as well as "Her Majesty's subjects" (Canadians) and Americans, could move freely between the borders for the purposes of trade and commerce. There were no border guards making you pull over your covered wagon to search under your animal skins and make you pay duty on flint muskets and trader's rum. Those were the days, huh?

In case you're thinking "Great, another benefit Indians get that we don't get," you'll notice that the Jay Treaty allowed free passage for Indians *and* the British and Americans. As it turned out, the Americans and British couldn't play nicely with each other for very long, so free passage between the borders was pretty much left to the Indians. Immigration policy in the US remains today that, "Native Indians born in Canada are therefore entitled to enter the United States for the purpose of employment, study, retirement, investing and/or immigration."

Not a bad deal and a pretty interesting fact, but what is the point of this little history lesson? When people hear about my Jay Treaty right, their first reaction is usually, "Man, you Indians got it good. The government gives you so many breaks." As if from day one the US and Canadian governments rescued us like birds with broken wings and nursed us back to health with special rights so that we may someday fly as equals to our non-Native counterparts.

Not even close! If you delve a little deeper into the actual history of the continent, you'll find that practically every Indian policy and so-called right was negotiated at a time when European powers relied heavily on Native people financially, militarily and politically. In the case of the first settlers, their reliance on Native people was literally for survival. So be careful what you believe about the first Thanksgiving—those pilgrims didn't bring much to that dinner except their appetites.

The point is the Jay Treaty was enacted primarily to serve the interests of American and Canadian trade by averting war and solidifying American independence. The reason the treaty included Native people is because First Nations were part and parcel to almost every aspect of the formation of America and were regarded as sovereign nations. The Jay Treaty was not a special right given to us out of the kindness of the US government's heart; it was negotiated with us because without our involvement, the US and Canada would not exist as we know it today—for better or worse.

Often when people hear about a special right like the Jay

Treaty, they will assume that *all* indigenous people share this right. In fact, special rights are assigned to indigenous people based on the category they belong to and more specifically what name is attached to that group. The Canadian constitution recognizes three Aboriginal groups: First Nations (Indians), Inuit and Metis. Each group has a different culture and heritage and is therefore assigned different rights. While First Nations may be the politically correct term used most frequently in Canada, the name has no legal bearing under the constitution. Those rights belong to "Indians," or more specifically "Registered Indians" or "Status Indians."

As I mentioned before, I am a Status Indian, which means I was issued a little red card that states I am "an Indian within the meaning of the Indian Act." There are many First Nations people who, for various reasons, do not possess this card and are not entitled to Jay Treaty rights. Inuit and Metis people are also not entitled to Jay Treaty rights as Status Indians because they are not officially recognized in the wording of the Jay Treaty as a "Native Indian born in Canada." The wording is pretty sticky, so it's important to remember that the legal and constitutional ramifications of naming this continent's first inhabitants go well beyond uptight political correctness.

To sum up, if I go to the border and introduce myself as a Canadian without mentioning my Indian status, and then proceed to tell them I am going to the United States for seven months to live and work, I will likely be ushered into that little room at the back of the station. Word of advice: never get ushered into that little room at the back of the station unless you have a fetish for latex gloves.

Legal terminology aside, the issue still remains of what is the properly accepted term. The confusion is understandable since not even we Natives can agree on what to call each other.

However, there are certain terms that even the most militant, camouflage-wearing, braid-sporting Native will grudgingly allow, depending on who's using it, in what context and if the user owes them money or not. Before we attempt to establish a term that is, at the very least, offensive to the fewest number of people, let's take a look at the controversy surrounding some of these names, starting with our old friend...

Indian

Remember the good ol' days when kids played a simple game of cowboys and Indians? Nowadays, due to political correctness you're more likely to find them playing a culturally sensitive game of "cattle technicians and Original Peoples." Oh, and kids aren't allowed to declare a loser anymore so unlike the real Wild West, everybody wins! Blah! Where's the shoot-em-up romance in that? When did the word "Indian" become so offensive? It's just a word, right? What's the big deal?

13

Well, in the case of "Indian" there is a lot of historical and legal baggage, but what may surprise you is that in many cases it's the "Indians" who don't want the word changed. So let's brush up on the whole Indian fiasco and see if the term is offensive, misunderstood or, as Goldilocks says, *Juusstt right*.

Here's a quick review of what we're taught in school: Christopher Columbus and two other boatloads of his homies sailed from Spain to find a trade route to India. He gets lost, lands in the Americas, calls the inhabitants "Indians" and the name sticks because everyone thinks it's cute until a bunch of "Indians" in the 1960s start getting uppity. I'm sure you've heard the protests that we are not from India so it is offensive to call us Indians. This statement often elicits the illuminating response, "Oh relax." For some reason, many non-Natives become enraged when it is suggested they shouldn't call us "Indians" anymore — as if choosing our own self-identification is equivalent to burning the flag. But Canadians are steeped in tradition and often reluctant to change, as evidenced in the fact that there is still a woman wearing a crown on our money.

For a long time it was generally accepted that the term "Indian" was bad and should be done away with immediately. Then a new theory surfaced amongst Native activists, academics and even stand-up comedians surrounding the origin of the word "Indian." This new theory suggested that Columbus's use of the word was an expression of reverence as demonstrated in this quote from the late, great George Carlin in his book, *Brain Droppings*:

> There's nothing wrong with the word Indian. First of all, it's important to know that the word *Indian* does not derive from Columbus mistakenly believing he had reached "India." India was not even called by that name in 1492; it was known as Hindustan. More likely, the word *Indian* comes from Columbus's description of the people he found here. He was an Italian, and did not speak or write very good Spanish, so in his written accounts he called the Indians, *Una gente in Dios*. A people in God. In God. In Dios. Indians.

Admit it, you read that passage in Carlin's voice, didn't you?

This theory was not only adopted by stand-up comedians, but also by scholars, writers and activists — and it still exists today even though it has been largely debunked. As author Cecil Adams has pointed out, the phrase *una gente in Dios* does not appear in any of Columbus's writings. Back in Greek and Roman times, there was evidence of the words "Indian" and "India" to describe "dot" not "feather" Indians long before Columbus got lost and was discovered by the people of the Americas. The words "India" and "Indian" are derived from the Indus River and appear in ancient Sanskrit writings. Martin Behaim's globe of 1492, which was created before Columbus's voyage, labels the region as India, not Hindustan. When Ferdinand and Isabella sent Columbus on his merry way they provided him with a passport written in Latin "toward the regions of India" (*ab partes Indie*). In Columbus's letters he frequently mentions India and Indians. The phrase *una gente in Dios* appears nowhere in his writings.

The reason I bring up the *in Dios* theory is because it illustrates how easily misconceptions about the history of Native people are accepted as fact even without tangible proof. However, I do understand why the *in Dios* theory is popular from a Native perspective. It's empowering to believe that our ancestors were so pure, so gentle and so beautiful, that even a colonizing force of invaders stood in reverence of these "people in God." Perhaps that *was* the reality of early Natives, and as a Native person I am persuaded to believe it, but the more you delve into the real history of Columbus, the idea that he had any reverence for these people is highly unlikely.

Volumes have been written about the treatment of Native people at the hands of Columbus and his crew. At first contact, Columbus recorded that the "Indians" treated the newcomers with extreme hospitality and charity. However, the Europeans regarded this kindness as ignorance and inferiority and immediately set about enslaving them, raping them and viciously slaughtering all those who attempted to defend themselves. On subsequent trips to the Americas, Columbus frequently kidnapped Indians to be brought back to Spain as slaves. Many of them did not survive the trip.

Bartolomé de Las Casas, among other observers, wrote sickening first-hand accounts of the savagery inflicted upon Natives by the colonists. It was not uncommon for European colonists to murder Natives by mass hangings, roasting them on spits, burning them in groups at the stake or hacking children into pieces to be used as dog food. For entertainment, some placed bets on who could slice a live Native man in two, cut off his head or disembowel him in one blow. The colonists also performed inhuman acts of cruelty and murder on Native babies that I won't even get into here.

If Columbus truly regarded the first people as "in God" then I would hate to see how he behaved during Sunday mass. To suggest that he was reverent of the people is to ignore that, from day one, Native people were often regarded as soulless chattel to be murdered and enslaved in the interest of European profit. When it comes to the Columbus myth, sometimes a cigar is just a cigar and sometimes people just get lost and think they're in India. Case closed.

So if there is no historical basis for the *in Dios* theory and many Native people find the term "Indian" offensive, why do so many Native people call themselves "Indian"? One answer is there is a sentimental attachment to the use of the word. It's a term that many older Natives have always used and just continue to use. It also persists through the act of reclaiming a pejorative name, much the same way that African Americans claim they are reclaiming the "n word." Finally, the word "Indian" holds a lot of legal and political weight that makes it difficult to abandon the term outright. The primary reason for its continuation in Canada can be attributed to the infamous Indian Act.

The Indian Act

Anyone who has ever read a newspaper or watched a news story about Natives in Canada has probably heard of the Indian Act, "an Act respecting Indians" (although I think that "respecting Indians" part is a bit misleading). The Indian Act was passed like a painful kidney stone in 1876, and confirms the Canadian government's full control over "Indians, and Lands reserved for the Indians" under the Constitution Act of 1867. The Act defines who can legally call oneself an "Indian" and establishes the legal rights and restrictions that Indians are subject to. In other words, the Indian Act was designed to tell Indian people what they *can* do, but mostly what they *can't* do.

On the plus side, the Indian Act also affirms that Indian rights are beyond legal challenge since they are entrenched in the Constitution Act of 1982. That "beyond legal challenge" part is why the Native community is reluctant to abandon the Indian Act altogether. There is also a fear in the Native community that changing the name "Indian" to something more PC may result in the dissolving of those rights attached to "Indians." If that sounds like Indians just being paranoid then you've obviously never spent five minutes with a policy lawyer when he is dissecting legalese.

17

Recently, the Department of Indian Affairs and Northern Development changed its name to Aboriginal Affairs and Northern Development, but the term "Indian" is still in the department's legal name and is still the legal term used in the Canadian constitution and federal statutes. Regardless of whether you use the word "Indian" or not, intent is everything, and if you're the type of person who snarls when you call someone an Indian and then spits on the ground, it's probably a good sign that you're not the type who can get away with using the word "Indian" in any circumstance.

Aboriginal

Put simply, Aboriginal is a blanket word that refers to three groups of indigenous people recognized in section 35 of the Canadian constitution: Indian, Inuit and Metis. Since each of the groups is governed in a different way, not all constitutional rights apply to each in the same way, even though they are all lumped together as "Aboriginal." In Canada, "Aboriginal" is used frequently to describe all indigenous Canadians but the rest of the world usually associates the word with indigenous Australians, who used to be called "Aboriginees." That's probably why whenever I hear the term Aboriginal I always picture Crocodile Dundee saying, "That's not an Aboriginal... *THAT*'s an Aboriginal." Hey, I never said I was impervious to stereotypes from other countries!

18

First Nations

"First Nations" is the most popular term in use right now to describe Native Canadians. Officially, the term applies to — you guessed it — Indians. Since the Inuit and Metis have distinct identities, they are not often referred to as First Nations. Although the Canadian government uses "First Nations" and "Aboriginal" as its formal descriptor, in all legal dealings the terms "Indian reserve," "Indian band" and "Indian land" are still the official terms used. Do you see a theme developing? That brings me to the one term (actually many terms) that 97.4% of the Native population will approve of.

Traditional Names

When I moved from Vancouver to Toronto, one of the first places I frequented was the Native Canadian Centre — or as my father's generation called it, the "Indian Friendship Centre." Unfortunately, not everyone at this Friendship Centre was very friendly. One day while I was speaking to some fellow First Inhabitants I innocently referred to myself as "Native." That word raised the ire of a woman standing nearby who hissed, "You are not *Native*, you are Anishinaabe!" Having just moved to Toronto from East Vancouver, I immediately assumed that "them was fighting words."

"What the hell did you call me!?" I barked back.

"We are the first people of this country," she said. "We are not Native, First Nations or Indian. YOU — are Anishinaabe!"

Although taken aback, I explained that I was from British Columbia and I had never heard the word "Anishinaabe" before in my life. I then went on to suggest that her insistence on calling all Native people "Anishinaabe" was just another form of oppressive, colonial Pan-Indianism. (Yeah, I had a mouth on me back then.) Needless to say, this went over like a smoke signal in a rainstorm. Her final words to me were something along the lines of that I was in Toronto, which is Ojibway territory, so I should have respect and use only Anishinaabe terms. End of conversation.

One year later, that woman became my wife... Nah, just kidding! What this story illustrates is the growing movement amongst Native people to be recognized by our pre-contact names. So if you think it's hard to use the proper term now, get a load of this: there are over 350 Native nations in Canada, each with its own name for its particular nation. Within those nations, there are different pronunciations of that name based on regions. For example, my people are known as "Shuswap," which was the name given to us centuries ago by non-Native linguists. Shuswap is a variation of our traditional name, which is actually "Secwepemc." The Secwepemc Nation is divided into southern and northern Secwepemc and the spelling and pronunciation of Secwepemc words varies depending on whether you are in the north or south. It would be like going to a party in California and saying the party was "totally gnarly," whereas in Massachusetts the same party would be "a wicked piss-ah." Same, but different.

I hope that cleared things up. So let's recap: in Canada, when choosing a name to refer to Natives, the most preferable is the traditional name from that region; however, the politically correct terms — First Nations, Aboriginal and sometimes Native — will generally suffice. At the bottom of the list is "Indian" and no amount of screaming about how you hate PC crap is going to change the negative connotations associated with that word over centuries. The word "Indian" is more or less done. Get over it. Now that I have said that, let's shake things up and look at the United States, where the word "Indian" is commonplace.

20

American Indian

"American Indian" can be found in treaties since the Pilgrims arrived and started sewing buckles into their hats for God knows what reason. To this day, all branches of the US government still use the term as an official descriptor. However, it wasn't until the American Indian Movement was founded in 1968 that the term became widely used. A 1995 study by the US bureaus of Labor Statistics and the Census found that about half of those who identify as indigenous prefer the term "American Indian." Only thirty-seven percent use the term "Native American" and the rest prefer other terms or had no preference. (Hey, maybe those "other terms" or "no preference" folks should call themselves Anishinaabe!)

"American Indian" usually refers to the indigenous people of the main part of the United States — or as the Alaskan Natives call it, "the lower forty-eight" (I like to call it "Canada's leaky basement"). The Alaskan Natives have their own system of government and set of rights so they do not refer to themselves as Native American, American Indian and especially not Anishinaabe. Speaking of Alaskan Natives...

Eskimo

The Alaskan Natives were once called "Eskimo" but that term is now cringe-inducing in the same way the word "Indian" is controversial in the lower forty-eight states. One theory is that the word was originally thought to be a slur because in Algonquian languages it loosely translates to "eaters of raw meat." This was long before it was fashionable to spend hundreds of dollars on raw sushi, so back then "Eskimo" was meant as an insult. Nowadays the word "Inuit" is most commonly used to describe the first peoples of northern Canada, Alaska, the Arctic and even eastern Siberia. So while "Alaskan Native" is the official term in the US and "Inuit" is the proper term in Canada, many of them still refer to each other as "Eskimo" the same way "Natives" refer to each other as "Indian." However, one thing you do *not* call an Alaskan Native/ Inuit/ Eskimo is "Indian." That's offensive. Still with me? Take a moment to fill out your scorecard if you are playing along at home.

21

Native American

"Native American" (or Native Canadian) is the term the armchair etymologists love to attack when they say, "I was born here, so I'm native too." Unfortunately, this annoying sentiment has been around for a few hundred years. Back in the 1800s, a group of Anglo-Saxon Protestant Americans started calling themselves "Native Americans" to suggest they were less immigrant than the recent Irish and German immigrants. That group then formed an anti-immigrant political party called the "Know-Nothings." The Know-Nothings also called themselves the "Native American Party" to signify that they were there first. I think the "Know-Nothings" is a more apt descriptor.

When the civil rights movement rolled around in the 1960s,

the term "Native American" became popular amongst activists who were uncomfortable with the use of the word "Indian" in "American Indian." The word "American" has also been questioned based on the long sordid history between Native people and the US government. The argument is that since Natives were not treated as if they were equal to regular Americans, why then would they adopt the term "American" as a descriptor? In addition, the Native people of America have constitutional protection as sovereign nations separate from the United States of America.

22

Indigenous

"Indigenous" is another word that some people love to jump all over to prove their smarty pants-ness. Indigenous basically means that something originates, or is naturally occurring, in a specific region like a plant, animal or person. The internet geniuses love to point out that since all land masses in the world supposedly broke off from one supercontinent called Pangaea, then nothing is really indigenous to North America. I disagree. One thing that is very indigenous to North America is annoying internet geniuses.

The United Nations uses the term "indigenous peoples" as an official descriptor for those "naturally occurring" people who existed on their land masses when they drifted away from Pangaea. However, the term is controversial for those who feel it does not reflect the history of First Peoples whose ethnicity was affected by European colonization or those who are descendants of migratory groups and do not technically qualify for the UN definition of "indigenous." There are also some non-indigenous people who argue that since Native people, *in theory*, originally came from Asia, they are not indigenous to North America. I say *in theory* because the "Indians from Asia" hypothesis is another notion that has been widely accepted as truth even though it is frequently scrutinized as new evidence presents itself.

Personally, I don't use the term indigenous because it just sounds dirty. I can't explain why, it just does. 'Nuff said.

Amerind

Another word that struggles to find acceptance in North America is the intellectualized "Amerind." The term is a mash-up of "American Indian" or "American" and "indigenous." This merger occurred in much the same way that tabloids blend the names of Hollywood couples like "Brangelina" or "Bennifer." The term was invented near the beginning of the twentieth century, and is now mostly used in Latin America. I have often witnessed people attempt to use this term around North American Natives only to be met with blank stares. Whenever I hear people use the word "Amerind" I am reminded of the scene in *Mean Girls* when Gretchen says, "That is so *fetch*," and Regina barks back, "Gretchen, stop trying to make 'fetch' happen!" That's right, I used *Mean Girls* to reference linguistic origins. You won't find that in any college anthropology syllabus.

Redskin/Red Indian

While this term may seem like a no-brainer, it is shocking how many non-Natives will insist it is perfectly acceptable. One of the arguments is that Native people also use it, as in the popular music group A Tribe Called Red or the response to the Trudeau government's White Paper by the Indian Chiefs of Alberta known as the "Red Paper." See!? Indian and red in one sentence, perfectly acceptable! What most fail to realize is that the use of the word "red" is often used ironically to reclaim colonial terminology. Don't let the old western movies fool you; we Natives are quite adept at irony. Besides, there isn't a single Native person who would actually describe his or her skin colour as red—Native people are adamant that they are immune to sunburn.

The term redskin was used throughout the eighteenth and nineteenth centuries. Variations of redskin were also used to describe the people of India or, as I like to call them, "the people who stole our name." Uses of the phrase *redskin*, *red Indian* or *red man* are found in writings as far back as the 1580s. There are multiple theories about how the word came to be, one being that it was just another way to describe different ethnicities based on skin hue like "white" for Caucasians and "black" for Africans. Harmless enough—although I wonder why "Indian Red" was removed from crayon boxes and why there were no crayons called "Caucasian White" or "African Black." Another theory, and the one that most people cite as reasons for its acceptability, is that "red Indian" described the Beothuk people of the Maritimes who covered their bodies with red clay and red ochre. The Beothuk people are now extinct, so I guess we'll never know.

Regardless of the theoretical origins of the word, it is now considered an extremely offensive term, similar to the "n word" for African Americans. After hundreds of years of being called *expletive* redskins, you would be hard-pressed to find many Natives who believe the slur is a reference to ochre-covered Beothuks. Heck, even the "n word" has its origins in a non-offensive Latin context, but words evolve and the "n word" is bound to be cut from any movie you watch on an airplane. This is why there is so much controversy (and subsequent eye-rolling) over the team name "Washington Redskins"; and yes, I will add my two cents on that rigmarole later.

Savage

It may (or may not) be hard to believe that anthropologists once referred to all of the world's indigenous people with the word "savage." For example, in the 1920s the famous anthropologist Bronisław Malinowski published a study entitled *The Sexual Life of Savages*. (That book sounds hot! Eat your heart out, Jackie Collins.) As western expansion stretched across North America, the US and Canadian governments frequently referred to Aboriginal people as "savages" in official documents. Its use was frequently associated with the fact that many Native people at that time were not yet Christians and were therefore "savages." So while the term may have been an *official* term at one time, it is now *officially* offensive. A similar name given to Native people based on their perceived lack of Christian religious beliefs is "heathen." I have heard sneaky non-Natives try to get away with using this one by saying things like, "He went to the bank. *Heathen* went to the store." Nice try, I'm onto you!

Squaw

Like redskin, squaw is one of those words folks will insist is not offensive because its historical origin is innocent. They can argue that at their own peril, since it is now considered the most derogatory word you can call a Native woman. Nevertheless, there are still people in North America and throughout the world who received their education about Native peoples from Hollywood westerns and still believe "squaw" is the proper term for Indian women. One of the arguments for its acceptability is that there is no pejorative association in terms like squawfish or squawberry. Now if you were to design a doll that looked like a little Native girl and called it Squawberry Shortcake, we would have a huge problem.

In the most truncated historical sense, the word "squaw" comes from an Algonquian word that loosely translates to mean "woman." This fact is cited in numerous writings from people of the Massachusetts tribes, who lived in what is now called Hawaii. (Just kidding. They lived in Massachusetts—I was just seeing if you were paying attention.) Many languages of the Algonquian family and other eastern regions have variations of words for women that have spun off into the word "squaw." Evidence of the word began to appear in English as Europeans mixed with those eastern tribes. In recent years another theory has come to light, reported by linguist Ives Goddard, that the intent behind the word "squaw" derives from the Mohawk word "ojiskwa," which translates politely as "vagina." The basis for the argument that "squaw" was used as a slur came from the belief that missionaries and trappers would describe Native women using the word "squaw" (in the vagina sense) to dehumanize them. The evidence of this is sketchy, but it does lend credence to the offensive nature of the word as it is used today.

Regardless of the origin of the word, it has now morphed into a derogatory term. For those who feel they need to "educate" Indians on the true meaning of the word, we get it. It's a fascinating historical fact, but when a Native woman is walking home and a car full of boys scream "Squaw!" at her, you can be damned sure it is not in reference to the original Algonquian meaning. Maybe the word was innocent in the 1600s, but it sure as hell isn't now. Don't use it!

Indian Princess

The concept of the Indian princess is a misnomer because Natives in North America did not perceive their leaders in terms of hierarchical royalty. The act of referring to chiefs as kings, and their daughters as princesses, began with newly arrived Europeans who did not grasp the complex systems of Native government and imposed their European understanding of government on Native tribes, i.e. royalty that ruled over subjects.

In addition, some European explorers were bound by international decrees that they could only negotiate land deals with sovereign leaders like kings and queens. When they came into contact with Native tribal leaders, the European negotiators would call them kings or queens so they could engage in territorial negotiations that would be recognized by European courts. Although Native tribal governments seldom resembled the monarchies of Europe, the titles stuck, most notably in the first Indian Wars and to the Native leader Metacomet, referred to as King Philip by the English. The daughters of these so-called kings and queens were therefore referred to as Indian princesses.

Real-life historical figure Pocahontas was the daughter of a chief and is often mistakenly referred to as an Indian princess. She is also included among the list of fictional Disney princesses such as Cinderella, Snow White and Sleeping Beauty — strange company to keep, considering that Pocahontas didn't marry John Smith and didn't live happily ever after. She died in England of unknown causes, possibly of disease or even poison. Now that's a ride I would love to see at the magic kingdom!

Nowadays many Native Nations will hold gatherings or competitions where they will choose a woman to represent their culture and will crown her a tribal or Indian "princess." These titles are mostly pageant-oriented the way you would name somebody a beauty "queen," and should not be misconstrued as any sort of tribal power. I wish someone had explained that to my ex-girlfriend, who won an Indian princess competition and immediately tried to send me to the guillotine.

Papoose

Another word the Algonquians gave us was *papoòs*, which also loosely translates as "child." But it is another word that people incorrectly believe is used by all Native people. According to linguists, the word can be traced to the Narragansett tribe of Rhode Island and became popular when Roger Williams recorded it in his 1643 book *A Key into the Language of America*. Using the word papoose is not something most Indians automatically do. Based on my experiences as a Native child, I was more often referred to as "Put that down!" "Don't eat that!" and "Go to your room!" I know these names were not derived from Native words, but they sure spoke to the point.

28

LET'S RECAP AGAIN: *INDIAN* IS USED AMONGST NATIVE people but often reluctantly. There are legal reasons for its continued use but it is generally considered offensive if used out of context and by non-Natives. In the United States, *Native American* or *American Indian* is considered appropriate though it depends on whom you are talking to and how they feel about America as a concept. *Indigenous* is way too broad a term and *Amerind* is "fetch" but not in a good way. In Canada, *Aboriginal* and *First Nations* are the commonly used terms that you can usually get away with and not raise the ire of most Native people. They also happen to be the two words most often used for official purposes. For best results, try to call Native individuals by their *original name in their original language*. There are over 350 of these names in Canada alone, so if you want to go this route, you should start cramming.

What have we learned so far? There are many names used for our people because not all of us can agree on one. We all have our own pasts, world views and prejudices that will inform the term we prefer. As a result, there will never be one term that pleases one hundred percent of Natives all the time. Sorry. Luckily, Native people have a reputation as some of the most open, accepting and forgiving people in the world. Using an improper PC term will usually be ignored as long as your conversation is respectful and comes from a place of friendship. However, suggesting that a Native person should not be offended by a term and offering up a linguistics lesson to prove your point does not erase the fact that those words have been used to demean and lessen Native people for centuries.

Maybe you're still wondering why there are so many politically correct names for us? The short answer is: every name that we have been given has been used as an insult at some point in history; we're just trying to find one that not even our haters can use offensively. In the meantime, I am going to use a number of different terms throughout this book to describe my people, and I can get away with it — because I'm an INDIAN.

NATIVE PERCEPTIONS

THE EUROPEAN P.O.V.

"Walk like an In-di-an"

WHENEVER LAUNDRY DAY ROLLS AROUND AND I'M wearing jeans and a T-shirt, and not my regular apparel of feathers and buckskin, my appearance will often elicit the response, "You don't look Native—you look Hispanic or Italian or Portuguese." I have heard this repeatedly since I cut off my waist-long hair many moons ago. Back when my follicles were flowing there was never any question about my Native heritage, but now that I am neatly shorn it seems the only people who recognize me as Native are other Natives and the police (I wish I were joking about the police part).

When pressed to clarify what a "real" Native looks like, the description is fairly predictable: high cheekbones, dark skin, long black hair and a nose that is squared and sloped. Apparently all "real" Natives look like the logo for the Chicago Blackhawks. Although there are hundreds of different First Nations across the continent with their own specific look, culture and style of traditional dress, the image that most people view as authentically Native can be summed up in three words: *Dances with Wolves*. There is also a high percentage of individuals whose description of a "real Native" would contain far less noble descriptors.

When I was a young actor performing in a play in Edmonton, I ventured out to a karaoke bar one night with two of my Native cast-mates. Almost immediately, a well-imbibed Caucasian man sat down with us and asked what race we were. We all responded "First Nations," but our intoxicated friend was having none of it. Through bleary eyes he looked at my cast-mates and said, "You guys are 'iffys,' but..." he pointed to me, "you're Chilean!" We reiterated that we were all of Native descent but the man persisted. "You guys aren't Native, I know Natives. I used to work at a liquor store and..." Before he could finish, his friend quickly grabbed him by the shoulder and yanked him out of the bar into the cold Alberta night.

While this may seem like an isolated redneck incident, a majority of Native people have described similar experiences of not being considered Native unless they fit into one of two categories: the long-haired romantic icon on horseback, or the miscreant lingering outside the liquor store begging for treaty reparations. As a result, when people finally discover someone is Native after years of personal contact at a normal job, playing a normal game of golf, mowing a normal lawn and enjoying a normal glass of Chardonnay, they will normally respond, "I thought you were Spanish or Italian or Portuguese." The statement is rarely uttered with malice, but we Natives hear it so often that the subtext always feels the same: "Natives don't do normal things. I know Natives. I used to work at a liquor store...."

Even if you've never worked at a liquor store or even met a real live Indian, when the terms "First Nations" or "Native American" come up you probably have an image that immediately springs to mind. I'm willing to bet that initial image does not include the words "investment banker," even though there are countless Natives out there that are very successful at managing your RRSPS or Roth IRAS or SPCAS, or whatever the heck they manage (obviously, I am not one of those successful Native investment bankers). You will often hear Native people complain about our portrayal in the media, which usually manifests itself in one of two ways:

1) As a romantic symbol of a bygone era, like when the government trots us out to dance in our regalia at the Olympics.

32

2) In numerous documentaries that explore everything from substance abuse to government corruption to incest. In the Native community, these documentaries are frequently referred to as "poverty porn."

I'm not suggesting that these depictions are entirely inaccurate. The traditional songs, dances, artwork and rituals displayed in those opening ceremonies are still practised today with the same regard as our pre-contact ancestors granted them. However, there is a commonly held belief from outside the Native community that we are holding onto remnants of the past in a last-ditch attempt to cling to our vanishing heritage. In fact, modern Native spirituality and traditions are as powerful and redemptive to those who practise them as any Eastern or Western religion from around the world. Unfortunately, these practices are often disregarded as quaint or rustic, belonging to an era when Native people still lived in teepees and were considered "real Indians."

Today, the images of Native artwork, Native crafts and Native dancers are often used by Canada and the United States to promote tourism. Ironically, up until a generation ago the Canadian and US governments outlawed Native religion and cultural practices and imprisoned people for practising the customs that they now advertise as a proud aspect of our North

American heritage. To paraphrase the Virginia Slims ads, "You've come a long way, Papoose."

On the other hand, the representation of Native people surrounded by crime and living in squalid conditions is often attributed to the loss of those historic traditions through the legacies of residential schools and forced relocation. There are many Natives and non-Natives who believe that returning to a land-based, traditional way of life is the only way to free First Nations people from destitute conditions on reserves and in cities. There is also a number of Natives and non-Natives who believe the only way to reverse the damage inflicted upon First Nations by the dominant society is to — are you ready for this — *fully assimilate* into that dominant society.

When it comes to solving the societal woes of Native people, the perception is rarely that there is a middle ground. Historic Natives are romanticized because of their refusal to assimilate into encroaching white society, while modern Natives are vilified because of their refusal to assimilate into encroaching white society. In both cases, Natives are often perceived as the "other," unable to reconcile their ancestral heritage with the complexities of society.

This Indian "other" theme is often at the centre of movies in which the main character is a contemporary Native. The tagline for these films is usually a variation on the phrase *torn between two worlds.* The Native character is almost always someone from a reservation who goes to the city, ends up on skid row and through some mystical device (a wizened elder, an animal spirit guide or a sudden vision) realizes the city is not for him and immediately returns to his reservation where he belongs. The final credits roll over the sound of drums and Native flutes and everyone weeps with joy because the Indian is roaming free in his natural habitat.

I've read hundreds of scripts with this exact same premise. Heck, I've even written one or two. What is so amusing about this city-ain't-no-place-for-an-Indian theme is that, according to recent statistics, more than half of all Native North Americans reside in urban centres. It's true: we live among you. We park your cars, we manage your money, we fight in your armed forces and yes, we date your daughters (cue scary music now). What's even more important to note is that many of these urban Natives have managed to strike a healthy balance between maintaining their ancestral traditions and being productive members of society. And that includes paying taxes—WHAAAAT!? More on that later.

Whether your image of a "real Indian" is of the "noble savage" or the "drunken criminal" variety, it's important to note that in both cases the perception of what a real Indian is, or looks like, is the result of hundreds of years of fear-marketing and commodification of the Native image. I'm not saying that every stereotype about Native people is false; I am saying that the majority of stereotypes that do exist have largely been manipulated, exploited and sometimes blatantly lied about to further the interests of those individuals whose interests need to be furthered.

Hold on, hold on! Before you throw this book on the pile of conspiracy manifestos, I assure you I am far from being a tinfoil-hat-wearing, bunker-stocking paranoid who blames the government and Illuminati for every Aboriginal social problem. Nor would I ever deny that Native people are partly responsible for enforcing the clichés that contribute to our overblown misrepresentations. However, when you dig a little deeper into the history of this continent and examine the intent behind the images associated with Native people, you'll find that they are frequently structured to serve the needs of two words: "trade" and "commerce." It's also important to note that the constructed images we have of Native people today have remained virtually unchanged over five hundred years.

First Contact

Before we continue, I want to assure you that I am not a Columbus basher. If it weren't for him we wouldn't have Columbus Day in the US and I wouldn't be able to buy appliances for sixty percent off. I also want to assure you that this is one of the last times I'll mention his name in this book. However, in order to understand how modern-day images of Native people began, we have to consider the European perspective on Native people and Native societies from the time of first contact. Thus, we begin with our old friend Christopher Columbus, since there are few documented writings from Leif Ericsson, who was actually the first European to have landed in the Americas hundreds of years before Columbus. That's right folks, just like every Winter Olympics, Norway always comes first.

When Columbus first arrived and he and his sailors came ashore in the Bahamas, the Arawak Natives greeted them with food, water and gifts. Columbus was shocked and noted in his log that the Natives were willing to trade practically all of their possessions, as if the accumulation of material goods had no bearing whatsoever on the goodness of a person's character. I know, right, what a bunch of commie pinkos! Columbus also wrote that the Natives were "well-built, with good bodies and handsome features...." (That "handsome features" part is one stereotype that I don't think any Native would attempt to debunk.)

Columbus then goes on to mention how the Natives would make awesome slaves and easy converts to Christianity, as mentioned in the previous chapter. These descriptions of the Arawaks would be repeated countless times over the years by European settlers to describe all the Indians of South and North America, who were also noted to be hospitable and eager to share. Such traits were not common in Europe during the Renaissance, which was dominated by religion, royalty and an insatiable desire for money.

In 1492 when Columbus sailed the ocean blue and landed on the shores of "Not India," Spain was in the process of becoming the first world power. The fall of Granada had just put an end to over seven hundred years of Islamic rule. The Spanish Inquisition was underway and resulted in the execution of an estimated three thousand to five thousand people and the expulsion of any Jews or Muslims who failed to convert. The Spanish Inquisition was eventually brought to the Americas, where Inquisitors read from decrees that declared that if Natives did not convert to Catholicism they would immediately be beheaded. The decrees were read in Spanish, which the Natives did not understand, so even a fear-based conversion was not possible. As a result, while the Renaissance movement was occurring back in Europe, in the Americas there was a movement of bloodshed, plunder, rape and human trafficking, all in the name of European religion, trade and "civilization."

It should come as no surprise, then, that Columbus and his counterparts naturally regarded these hospitable and docile people who greeted them as uncivilized, considering the European definition of civilization at the time. The Natives did not have religion (as the Europeans understood it); they did not have weapons (as the Europeans understood them); and they gave away almost as much as they kept (the Europeans definitely didn't understand that). This disconnect between the First Nations and European world views has been an endless source of derision that still exists today.

So right from the get-go, Native people were dismissed as inferiors and slaves because of their lack of Christian faith and supposed inability to accumulate wealth: two attributes that were of paramount importance to European society at that time. As more Europeans arrived, there was a growing sentiment that Natives were primitive and in desperate need of superior European religion, technology and medicine in order to save them from themselves. The irony is that European medicine at that time consisted primarily of bloodletting, and every new wave of early immigrants reported nearly perishing if it weren't for Native technologies (such as housing, medicine and sustenance practices). Yet, if you spend just a few moments surfing the internet you will come across innumerable posts that portray Natives as rooting around in their own filth until the Europeans came, wiped the crust from their eyes and gave them all Xboxes.

As a young Native student in the Canadian school system, I was inundated with images of my primitive and Neanderthalian ancestors in textbooks and artists' renderings on the walls of my school. In early history courses there were always sections on the First Peoples of North America, which only took a couple of days to teach. These lessons consisted of an overview of Native shelters, Native hunting patterns and Native food-gathering techniques that early Natives relied on to subsist and survive (which is seemingly all they did back then). If the school was particularly liberal it would even have an arts-and-crafts day where students could take their new-found knowledge of these primitive people and build teepees out of Popsicle sticks, or longhouses slapped together from pieces of tree bark. The students would then decorate these Native habitats with differently coloured sparkles, or stickers of unicorns and Hello Kitty. You know, just like my ancestors used to do it.

And then, like the mysterious Aztecs of centuries ago, the Natives just disappeared. In the years of history lessons that followed, I was inundated with tales of European civilization, of great feats and victories of European rulers, heroic tales of European pioneering and westward expansion, and the hard-fought establishment of European democracy that would forge this continent to make it the envy of the world it is today. Forever and ever, amen.

There is no mention of Native people during this epic period, save for the occasional incident where they attack a fort with their primitive weapons and attempt to slow the inevitable wheels of progress. It would seem that during this time Native people were just sitting around campfires in Popsicle-stick teepees, clinging to their outdated and primitive ways while staring dumbly at the European advance on *terra nullius*. This stereotype has left an indelible mark on generations of schoolchildren and has formed the persistent image of Native people as sideline observers of the "civilization" of this continent. As we are taught in school, Native people were too primitive, too superstitious and too busy chasing game across the Bering Land Bridge to be of any real consequence.

38

The word "primitive" is used a lot in describing Native people, their communities and their systems of government. This is often because they are placed in contrast to European societies and in fact, many textbooks state that indigenous cultures were not as advanced as European society at that time. They then go on to list all the things that Europe had that Native societies didn't. Every so often they gave us a mulligan and said, "Some Native societies had farming cultures," but the statement is usually qualified by adding that they were nothing like the *great* farming cultures of Europe. Descriptions of the Indians of yesteryear often focus on nomadic tribes like the Plains Indians to provide a Pan-Indian description of all Native societies. These nomadic tribes are also the image that is most often marketed and upheld as the standard by which all Natives lived, and should have lived, from a romantic perspective.

The allegation that Native people did not have the same sophisticated infrastructures as Europeans is baffling because it's actually a complete and utter... well, I'm not going to say "lie." Let me just put it this way: when it comes to teaching about the Native people of North and South America, it's not what has been said about Native people (there has been very little), it's what has been omitted about Native people that has led to a very skewed version of the formation of this continent. Little if nothing is mentioned of the advanced Mesoamerican civilizations that predated European arrival by at least three thousand years. Textbooks insist that Europeans brought civilization to the Americas, when in fact pre-Columbian cultures are responsible for great advances in pyramid construction, math, engineering, astronomy, fine arts, medicine, agriculture and theology. They also employed advanced methods of metalwork using silver and gold long before Europeans arrived and supposedly "civilized" the Natives. In addition, pre-Columbian calendars were so accurate that when the Maya calendar ended a few years ago, survivalists were elated because they could finally tuck into their stockpiled canned goods from their underground bunkers.

39

These Native societies also invented the wheel, but some "experts" insist it was used only as a toy, probably because the gold standard of civilization is measured by the advent of the wheel. To suggest that Natives had a wheel but didn't know how to use it constructively allows historians to hold on to the last shred of evidence that these people were not as advanced as European civilizations, despite all evidence to the contrary. Mesoamerican cities were among the largest in the world, and the Maya constructed some of the most elaborate cities on the continent. Around 1500 AD, the Aztecs had built a wealthy empire of over ten million people. When conquistadors arrived in the Aztec capital, Tenochtitlan (on what is now modern-day Mexico City), they described its market as the largest they had ever seen. The Inca civilization ruled over roughly six to twelve million people and their cities were engineering marvels built over mountainous terrain with scientific precision and magnificent stonework. To connect the empire, the Inca built a system of roads that stretched over thirty thousand kilometres. There is even evidence of successful brain surgery in Inca civilization. That's right, folks: successful brain surgery!

Comparatively, in Europe at that time medicine was limited to exorcising supernatural forces and balancing the "four humours" (black bile, yellow bile, phlegm and blood). Doctors would try to cure sick patients by making them drink liquids made of mercury and sulphuric acid in order to balance the humours. The more violently the patient reacted to the treatment, the more the doctors believed it was working. Increased vomiting, diarrhea and uncontrollable bladder activity were also considered really good signs. Sometimes doctors would stick hot, burning plasters to a patient's body in order to make them sweat the sickness out. However, the most common treatment at that time was bloodletting, and it was used for practically every ailment. Break your leg? Open a vein. Got cramps? Cut your stomach open. Feeling a little depressed? Drain some blood. Most doctors believed that "bad blood" was responsible for almost every disease and malady that could afflict the human body.

40

I reiterate: back in the Americas — successful brain surgery! Alright, 'nuff said about that. When discussing medical innovations we rarely hear about the game-changing pharmaceuticals introduced to the world by Native North Americans, including quinine, ipecac and novocaine, which was brought back to Europe to treat malaria and marked the beginning of modern-day pharmacology. Instead we are told that it was European medicine that prevented death and sickness amongst Native tribes, an odd statement considering that estimates place the First Nations population in North America at around five million until European diseases arrived and reduced the population to mere thousands. It would appear that until European arrival, Native medicines and medical practices kept the First Nations populations quite healthy, thank you very much. We also don't hear that European medicines were often useless in saving Europeans from their own diseases, who instead relied heavily on natural immunities built up from centuries of living in overcrowded and disease-ridden centres of Europe. The fact that Native people lacked immunity to these diseases is often used to suggest a Darwinian-like Native weakness, as if Natives only had themselves to blame for not living in a constant state of filth and pollution.

Rarely in discussing Native farming cultures in North America do we learn about the advanced waterways, irrigation systems and genetic splicing of seed and crops that has informed farming and bioengineering techniques to this day. Or that many of the fruits and vegetables sold today originate from the discovery and cultivation of North and South American First Nations cultures.

41

The list of early Native accomplishments in engineering, politics, democracy, art and social equality goes on and on and is well documented by European historians. However, we never hear about these realities because North America was supposedly built on the principles of tolerance, religious freedom, equality and the pursuit of happiness. The fact that Native people were constantly denied all of these rights is never explained as a failure on the part of North American society — heaven forbid — but rather on the inability of Native people to grasp these concepts and be liberated from their primitive ways. If we were taught that many early Europeans relied on Native people for survival, respected Native people and in many cases emulated them, we would then have to re-examine the notion that civilization was brought to the New World, when in fact, civilization was already here. We would then have to admit that the atrocities that occurred in the ensuing centuries cannot be easily dismissed as well-intentioned attempts to civilize the uncivilized, but rather as an attempt to erase the involvement of an equally civilized people in the development of this continent. But hey, the textbooks are already printed and they're really expensive to change, so whatta ya gonna do?

The Good, the Bad and the Iffys

The image of the uncivilized, primitive Native is very much embedded in the psyche of modern North Americans. The original descriptions of Natives by that Italian guy who sailed from Spain but whom I promised not to mention anymore has stood the test of time as a sort of romanticized ideal Native. In other words, when non-Natives imagine the perfect Indian they usually have the same image that "he who shall not be named" wrote about in his log: a people with "good bodies and handsome features" and, most importantly, a desire to share and co-operate fully with white people.

42

In literature and movies, this sentiment has been portrayed countless times in the form of the Indian adoption story, where a white man is accepted into a tribe and immediately becomes a full-fledged Indian. In these Eurocentric narratives, the white person is usually a more valuable member of the tribe because of his advanced European heritage. The white man is a superior fighter to his Indian adoptees, he achieves Native spiritual nirvana almost overnight due to his superior European spirit, and tribal skills that take a lifetime for the average Indian to learn are mastered by the white man in just a few short months. Oh, and in every single case, the beautiful Indian maiden will forsake all Native men for this European male and gladly sacrifice her life for him.

This cliché of the European über-Native is not limited to North America. In the movie *The Last Samurai*, Tom Cruise is accepted into a tribe of samurais in Japan and as a result of his superior cavalry training (barf), he easily masters the art of samurai (an art of incredible discipline and lifelong immersion) and defeats every samurai in his path until he and only one other Japanese guy are left as the last samurai. In the blockbuster movie *Avatar* we learn that the white American hero is the only hope in saving the entire planet of Pandora from evil industrialists — proving once again that even in outer space, a white paraplegic armed with only a video game is more qualified to save the day than the indigenous Na'vi.

These stories of superior Europeans dominating primitive tribals occur all over the world, in locations such as Africa, Asia, India and pretty much anywhere European influence has spread. So while the ideal image of a Native person is of a proud and noble "other," the Native must also be willing to fully cooperate with and embrace the white man in order for his image to be palatable to the masses. It is also generally accepted that while the white man may learn from the Natives, it is the Natives who benefit the most from their adopted white son.

On the flip side is the image of the savage, drunken, rapist Indian. These Natives are usually depicted as such because they are uncooperative and antagonistic toward white people, traits that will inevitably lead to their demise. This image became prominent during the time of western expansion, when development was met by resistance from Native people whose homelands were decimated by land grabs and the advance of the railway through their territories. As more and more resistance from Natives occurred, more and more narratives surfaced that described the resistors as bloodthirsty, soulless creatures who thought nothing of murdering and raping innocent homesteaders in unimaginable ways — or at least in ways as unimaginable as the Spanish did to the first Natives.

It was a brilliant marketing technique, since it enabled developers and governments to deflect attention away from broken treaties, human rights violations and illegal business dealings, and focused their supposed cause on bringing religion, European-style democracy and general civilization to an un-Christian, uneducated and savage people. The marketing worked, and the move to bring light to this dark world of savage Indians was widely supported in hopes that they would become more like their acceptable counterparts: the Indians who co-operated with white people in strengthening trade and commerce in North America. In the days of the Old West, the frequently used descriptions for these two types of Natives were "friendlies" and "hostiles." I'm going to be a little coarser and suggest a different label for these two perceptions of Native people: Good Indians and Bad Indians.

In the days of the Hollywood western, circa John Wayne, John Ford and all the other Johns, the Indians were almost always "Bad." They were ignorant, cowardly drunkards who attacked women and children and shot innocent pioneers in the back. As the years went on, Hollywood became more liberal and the portrayal of the old-time Indian became more sympathetic. However, certain themes remained unchanged. In the newer westerns, the "Good" Indians are willing to work with the white man because they are smart enough to realize that co-operation is the only way to save their vanishing people. The Good Indians in these stories live in harmony with nature and never engage in sinful un-Christian behaviour.

The Bad Indians are the mortal enemies of the Good Indians and therefore the enemies of white people. They would rather face extinction than co-operate with the white man to save their vanishing people. When the Bad Indians inevitably capture a white man, the white man will use his superior intellect to outsmart the Bad Indians who are usually too drunk to notice that he has escaped. Or he will use his superior fighting skills to beat down not one, not two, but an entire village of Bad Indians. The Bad Indians are usually lust-filled, slothful drunkards who engage in strange customs involving slow torture, cannibalism and sexual deviance. Basically, the Bad Indians are the Old West version of a modern college fraternity.

Appearance-wise, you can always tell the Good Indians from

44

the Bad Indians in the newer Hollywood westerns. The Good Indians have "good bodies and handsome features" and are usually sporting long, flowing hair. The Bad Indians are ferocious and scarred and are usually sporting mohawks. Examples of the Good Indian/Bad Indian stereotype can be found in movies such as *Dances with Wolves* and *The Last of the Mohicans* (where again, it's a white man who is one of the last Mohicans). This cliché of the long-haired Indian versus short-haired Indian is the equivalent of the white hat/black hat cliché of the Hollywood cowboy.

Today, this Good Indian/Bad Indian stereotype is well embedded into the consciousness of non-Natives. You will often hear folks ask, "Why can't Indians move into the twenty-first century? Why can't they get off the reservations and become productive members of society? Why can't they stop drinking and sponging off the government and start paying taxes like the rest of us?" Modern resistance movements like Idle No More, the Oka conflict and the standoff at Wounded Knee are frequently met with the dismissive response, "We already give them way too much, when are they going to start being grateful and learn to co-operate?" In other words, when will they start being Good Indians?

45

Regardless of whether a Native is co-operative, there is a stigma attached to modern Natives as the "other" whose usefulness in society depends on how much or how little they co-operate with progress, trade and commerce. It is often baffling for members of the dominant society when they encounter Native people utilizing the mainstream system not to further assimilation, trade or commerce, but rather to further traditional Native causes. I mean c'mon, you're either a Good Indian or a Bad Indian; you can't be an "Iffy." Now that I have presented my version of the Good and Bad Indian, let's explore these labels as they relate to present-day stereotypes, which have created a whole new category of Indians known as, for lack of a better word, the Iffys.

NATIVE PERCEPTIONS

THE NORTH AMERICAN P.O.V.

"Our home and Native land?"

EVEN THOUGH RELATIONS BETWEEN NATIVES AND Europeans got off to a rocky start in the southern hemisphere, in Canada and the United States things were a little more co-operative at the outset—especially in Canada, where the weather and terrain were so extreme that early settlers had to adapt quickly to Indian civilization in order to survive. As a result, many Native women married European men who were then accepted into the wife's tribe. It was not as common for Native men to marry European women, who were usually only brought over if they were already married, or as potential wives for European pioneers. So while European men were willing to trade and intermarry with the Natives, European women were considered off-limits and only to be used for the purposes of European men—yet another notion that hasn't changed in over five hundred years.

Good Indians

Early on, the relationship between Natives and Europeans contained at least an outward appearance of co-operation and equality. Mind you, this was at a time when the European population was relatively small and relied heavily on Indians for survival, and for profit from the extremely lucrative fur trade. Back in Europe, fur hats were the epitome of chic and if you weren't sporting a fur chapeau then you wouldn't be able to get into any of the cool seventeenth-century discos. So Europeans in North America submerged themselves in Native society, learned Native trapping skills and spent so much time amongst Indians that they often became unrecognizable as Europeans—speaking mostly Native languages, wearing Native-style clothing and living in Native housing. These guys weren't just playing Indian, they were method-acting Indian.

47

In exchange for helping the Europeans get rich on fur, the Natives would get guns, steel traps and metallic cookware, which changed the traditional hunting and gathering practices of those Natives who did not come from a metallurgy tradition. I reiterate, many textbooks will suggest that white people introduced metallic goods (civilization) to the Americas when in fact metalwork and smelting techniques were used by many tribes long before Europeans arrived. Now that I got that piece of revisionist history out of the way, let's move on...

The point is, very early on the Natives and Europeans had a pretty equal relationship of *you scratch my back, I'll scratch yours* and correspondence back to Europe often stated that the Indians were amenable to helping European interests in the New World. In other words—say it with me class—they were *Good Indians*. Due to these glowing reviews, it was suggested that the co-operative Natives would easily convert to Christianity. So missionaries flocked to North America expecting the Natives to be waiting with open arms, desperate to be saved from their irrational and superstitious belief systems. Instead, the Natives proved to be reluctant converts and clung to their religion of balance, gratitude and social harmony rather than the new religion of talking snakes, wrathful Gods, and fire and brimstone. To the early Natives, Christianity seemed a little irrational and superstitious. Downright uncivilized, frankly. Nevertheless, the early missionaries dug in and as societal and financial woes befell the early Natives, the missionaries' position in the Native communities strengthened greatly. (Tee hee... I said "missionaries' position.")

Good Indians and the HBC

Anyone who has ever watched an episode of *Shark Tank* will know the two fundamentals of business are supply and demand. The Hudson's Bay Company and similar trading posts firmly established these precepts in early Native communities and created a situation that I like to call the *my Indian can beat up your Indian* phenomenon.

Once European goods were introduced into Native communities, the traditional social structures began to change. Native people relied on the fur trade to provide money and goods for their families and communities. As trade continued and spread across Indian territories, many communities became less focused on subsisting on their natural environment and more focused on gaining consumer goods. I know what you're thinking: "About time those long-haired pinko commie Indians added a little capitalism into their diet!" Except that the loss of Indian control over fur trade territories is largely regarded as one of the reasons for the eventual demise of the fur trade.

Don't worry, I'm not going to go into a long discussion about the fur trade. If you received your education in the Canadian school system you've probably had it up to your mink fur hats with the fur trade. However, it was an important part of European expansion in North America and established a very effective practice that still continues today: using Indians to fight your battles by controlling the supply and demand of their essential goods. Oh relax, I'm not ranting, that's Capitalism 101 and it's perfectly acceptable or, rather, *accepted*.

At the start of the fur trade, pelts were supplied mainly by Indian traders, especially the Huron and Odawa tribes. As the fur trade expanded, other tribes wanted in on the action and the Great Lakes region became a sort of Wall Street for the fur trade industry. Early on, the Winnebago tribes blocked the fur trade routes and the Odawa and Huron replied, "Oh no you di'int!" (I'm paraphrasing). They fought back and defeated the Winnebago, opening up the area for new tribes like the Sauk, Fox, Potawatomi and Ojibway. Then the Dakota Sioux attacked, the Huron and Odawa were driven out, and the Ojibway swooped in and fought with the Dakota for fifty years, etc... Round and round it went, tribe after tribe, all in the name of trade and commerce. Obviously, intertribal warfare occurred long before Europeans arrived, so this was nothing new, but the fur trade was unprecedented in that it was responsible for the mass migrations of Natives to a centralized location so they could stake their claims in this early version of the gold rush. Who said Indians don't have any entrepreneurial spirit?

While all this was going on, the Hudson's Bay Company became a monopoly and the majority of furs sold by Indians had to be brought all the way to Hudson Bay to trade. The HBC just had to sit back and watch the Indians fight each other and collect the furs from whoever was on top at the time. However, other businesses and individuals also moved in and started trading directly with the Indians, thereby undercutting the mighty HBC. As a result, the Hudson's Bay Company had to establish more outposts, which led to their competitors setting up even more out-posts, which led to the Hudson's Bay Company's merger with its competitor the North West Company. Eventually, the fur trade became so fractured with so many competitors and so many different trading styles and so many side deals and so many wartime embargos that the whole thing started to unravel.

Many historians suggest the fur trade really saw its glory days when Indians had control of the land and traded directly with Europeans. Many believe that the fur trade collapsed because of a lack of furs, but there were a number of times that furs were scarce and the industry still bounced back. Instead, the lack of Indian involvement in the trapping and maintaining of the industry is considered a major factor in the eventual demise of the fur trade. At any rate, by the time Europeans realized that fur hats were itchy and switched to silk hats, the nails were already pounding into the fur trade coffin.

The Royal Proclamation of 1763

The Royal Proclamation, which is often referred to as the "Indian Magna Carta," was introduced by King George III to stake out his claim on North America after Britain (*and Indians*) won the Seven Years' War. The Royal Proclamation officially established that Aboriginal people always held title to the land and would continue to hold that title until the land was negotiated away in a treaty. The Proclamation ensured that only the Crown could buy Indian land and private individuals were prohibited from engaging in any land transaction with Indians.

The Proclamation was designed to appease the Natives who were getting restless (see what I did there?) due to settler encroachment on their lands. Britain knew that Natives could threaten colonial settlement both legally and militarily, and when

Sir William Johnson addressed the Board of Trade in 1764 he warned that trying to overpower the Indians using force would result in defeat since "the Indians all know we cannot be a match for them in the midst of an extensive woody country." His contemporaries obviously agreed since they had already witnessed the strategic might of Aboriginal fighting forces.

For centuries the European, Canadian and American armies have learned a great deal about military strategy from First Nations people and have incorporated that knowledge into their numerous military campaigns. Ironically, in most of the major wars, North American battle strategies have utilized some variation of the strategy used by the Sioux, Cheyenne and Arapaho in defeating General Custer at Little Big Horn. Until Europeans and Americans learned how to fight like Indians, their armies basically just lined up in rows and charged at each other and whoever had the least amount of dead were the winners. So naturally, Sir William Johnson's words were heeded and the Canadian government instead decided to undertake a campaign of "purchasing the favour of the numerous Indian inhabitants" through the Royal Proclamation.

The Royal Proclamation also applied to the United States but as soon as the Americans declared independence from Britain they rendered it null and void. After the revolutionary war the Americans thought to themselves, *Injuns, we don't need no steenkin' Injuns*. Bad move. The US government was soon dogged by frontier violence with Indians and was forced to create its own version of the Royal Proclamation. In 1790 the US government passed the first in a series of Indian Intercourse Acts, which isn't as dirty as it sounds (get your mind out of the gutter). These acts, like the Royal Proclamation, prohibited settlers from unauthorized trade and travel on Indian lands. In 1823, the US Supreme Court further ruled that Indian land could only be purchased by the US government and not private individuals. Both the United States and Canada rightfully understood that without co-operation from Native people, they would not become the financial powers they are today (or rather, the great debtors to Asia they are today).

Since no law has overruled the Royal Proclamation, it is still upheld as a valid governing agreement in Canada. The Proclamation is also enshrined in section 25 of the Constitution Act of 1982, which guarantees that Aboriginal rights as defined in the Proclamation cannot be terminated or diminished. Interpretation of those rights is where the real disconnect between Natives and the Canadian government occurs. We'll get to that but first, back to the days of yesteryear.

Native people were such a powerful military force that most of the major battles fought in North America were won or lost through alliances made with them. Indians played crucial roles in battles like the Seven Years' War (known as the French and Indian War in the US), the American Revolutionary War and the War of 1812, to name just a few. Despite the fact Native people were often responsible for the major turning points in these battles, history books often describe these wars as being between European powers. This may seem like a small point considering that, technically, these countries were the ones that eventually planted their flags; however, the lack of Native recognition in the retelling of these wars is kind of like saying that the Second World War was fought and won solely by the Americans. If you were from Britain, Russia, Australia, Canada and every other ally country during the Second World War, you might get a little peeved at this revisionist history. That's exactly what it's like being Native and reading about the great "European victories" in North America. For the record, there *are* many Americans who swear the Second World War was won all by themselves. Just sayin'.

52

So how did alliances with Native people affect the European perspective of the early Indians? Well, as long as the Europeans and Natives were working together for a mutually beneficial purpose: making money on furs, making money on trade and making money through war, then Europeans thought Indians were just dandy. Don't get me wrong, many Europeans still looked down on Indians as inferior. In the eyes of many Europeans, Indians lacked a proper religion, a proper system of government and a proper sense of social propriety. However, the Indians proved to be an effective means to an end and not yet the obstacle they would later become.

53

Back then, Europeans regarded themselves as the spiritual, intellectual and social superiors to every other people on Earth. It would not stand for them to enter into trade or political agreements with lesser, primitive heathens, or even admit they were reliant on inferior Natives to reach their goals. If European colonization has taught us anything, it's that Europeans don't align themselves with savages — they take what is theirs and subjugate the indigenous populations. That couldn't happen in North America so instead the Europeans described the Native people as "noble," "loyal" and "virtuous"; terms normally associated with Europeans. However, the Natives were not yet Christianized so they were still considered "savages." On the other hand, the Indians who aligned themselves with opposing European forces were naturally perceived as bloodthirsty, ignorant dirtbags. But that's just a given.

After the War of 1812 when Canada and the United States had settled into their respective territories, they pretty much ran out of any use for their Indian allies. The Industrial Revolution began a push for rapid expansion into the West and the long-standing proclamations, treaties and alliances established in the early formation of North America became inconvenient obstacles in developing the continent, especially on legally protected Indian territories. So the Canadian and US governments began a new campaign of eliminating Native territories, sovereign status and tribal societies: the qualities that made the Indians such powerful allies during the days of trade and war in North America. Enter the missionaries, the booze slingers, the Indian agents and a fierce new marketing campaign that would turn all those formerly "Good Indians" into...

54 Bad Indians

While those Natives who co-operated with early Europeans were considered "Good Indians," there were some early settlers who were horrified by Indians from the get-go. The Puritans were especially mistrustful when they arrived in Plymouth in 1620, and their attempts to build numerous colonies on Indian land as well as convert Indians to Christianity by building "praying towns" eventually led to war between the colonists and the local Wampanoag tribe. During one of these wars, the Wampanoag leader Metacomet, or "King Philip" as he was referred to by the English, was betrayed and ambushed by a "praying town" Indian. Metacomet's severed head was displayed on a pike in Plymouth for over two decades. For hundreds of years Metacomet was portrayed as a demon while the Puritans were portrayed as doing God's work. One of the tools used to spread this propaganda was a book titled *Entertaining Passages Relating to Philip's War* by Benjamin Church, a captain present at Metacomet's ambush. An early printing of the book was published with a picture of Metacomet etched by Paul Revere. The image was an unflattering portrait of Metacomet as ugly, squat and pygmy-like.

Following their independence from England, Americans distanced themselves from their British roots by identifying instead with the first "Americans." The Pilgrims were the first to be described in mythical proportions, and Indians became a romantic symbol of the country's rugged and untamed past. Even Metacomet received an Oprah Winfrey–style makeover in 1827, when Benjamin Church's diary was reprinted, this time with a new engraving depicting Metacomet as tall, strong and heroic. The book still portrayed the early settlers as heroes, but it also turned Metacomet into a nineteenth-century version of *People's* "Sexiest Man Alive."

This type of schizophrenic marketing was common as North Americans struggled to find their identity. On one hand, they advertised the beauty of the untamed open wilderness while simultaneously encouraging newcomers to develop and tame that open wilderness. Although they marketed the Indians as an integral part of the rich history of North America, they also created narratives that portrayed Indians as bloodthirsty savages who required civilizing. At the beginning of western expansion, the Indians who co-operated with white settlers, or were no longer considered a threat, were labelled as "noble savages" while the Indians who resisted western expansion were called every expletive under the sun.

The first step in the propaganda machine was to paint the Indians as the "other." The alliances, friendships and territorial agreements that occurred between Europeans and Indians were quickly forgotten when it became clear the most desirable land for advancing white settlement was the land already occupied by the Natives. Remember, these were lands that were reciprocally agreed upon through legally binding treaties. However, after the US gained their independence, many Americans felt that the treaties negotiated with England should be ignored. In addition, there were numerous American Indian tribes that were loyal to Britain and had fought against the Americans during the Revolutionary

War. Awwwkward! Needless to say there was some bad blood so one of the first excuses for displacing the Indians was the commonly held sentiment, "C'mon, there's plenty of land for everyone, why are the Indians hogging it all?"—which is funny because that's eventually what the Indians thought about the white settlers.

The US government didn't really have any constitutional or legal standing to snatch up the lands from the Indians so they had to find their day's version of "weapons of mass destruction." This political leverage was achieved by attacking the character of the Indians: a people that had once been their allies and whom they previously armed to help fight their common enemy. Is any of this sounding similar to present-day wars overseas? As we saw from the Metacomet example, the white settlers were very good at picking and choosing when an Indian was heroic and when an Indian was a devilish shrivelled pygmy. In its marketing of Indians during the War of Western Expansion (herein known as WWE), the government chose the latter.

The white settlers identified with the image of the Puritan Pilgrims as brave new explorers, fleeing the tyranny of religious prosecution in England and arriving in Plymouth to make a life for themselves in peace and quiet. History omits that when the Pilgrims arrived on the shores of Plymouth, their entire modus operandi was religious persecution, and their life of peace and quiet consisted of building settlements on any piece of Indian land they saw fit. For the record, the first Thanksgiving wasn't a dinner of sharing and gratitude, it was an uneasy peace summit that would quickly deteriorate into war. The image we have now of Indians and Pilgrims dining together in unity was actually a PR stunt created by Abraham Lincoln during the Civil War to get the North and the South to sit down, shut up and just eat some turkey together.

The government also invented numerous excuses for why the

land and resources were ripe for the picking including: Indians didn't understand land ownership; Indians weren't developing the land and were wasting it; Indians weren't Christians and were therefore savages; and the most widely spread reason—Indians were bloodthirsty, murderin', raping devils, who were a threat to national security, and had to be removed, destroyed or assimilated. Whoa! Where did that come from!? I thought we were allies, I thought we were an integral aspect of the frontier spirit, I thought we were—oh, that's right, we were un-cooperative. "Bad Indians! Bad Indians! Go sit in the corner and think about what you've done!" And so the assault on Indian territories began. The government even used cavalry regiments to protect white settlers from the "Indian Problem."

57

In every conflict there will always be sympathizers (a.k.a. bleeding-heart liberals) and there were many white Americans in Congress and in American society who were sympathetic to the Indians. So when Indians started fighting back against encroaching white settlers, creating stories of Indian savagery was crucial in winning the hearts and minds of the American people. Businessmen, pulp fiction writers, congressmen, playwrights and advertising "mad men" all jumped on the chance to cash in on the popular good-vs.-evil tales of settlers and Indians.

Popular novelists like James Fenimore Cooper painted a picture of the West that was sympathetic to the eco-friendly version of the "noble savage" but also popularized the image of the "ignoble savage." In his classic tale *The Last of the Mohicans*, he painted the Good Indians (Uncas and Chingachgook) as brave and stalwart but the Bad Indian (Magua) as a savage, violent eater of raw meat. Man, raw meat really got a bad rap back then!

Stories like this, in which the depiction of Good Indians and Bad Indians are cut and dry, were common amongst writers who had never known any Native Americans or even researched

Native American societies. To give you an indication of how popular and overdone these stories were in the Old West, it would be like combining all the present-day movies, TV shows and books about zombies, vampires and comic book superheroes all into one genre. Yes, that many!

Captivity Stories

One of the more fascinating genres of Bad Indian narratives are the captivity stories because they unintentionally said more about white society than the Native societies they claimed to describe. Captivity stories were around long before Europeans arrived in North America but whether they took place in Africa, India or anywhere else that Europeans colonized a people, the themes were always the same. In the North American captivity stories, if a white man is captured he is forced to endure horrific torture at the hands of the savage Indians. He is tied to a post, covered in fire ants, relieved of his fingernails, forced to run through gauntlets of short-haired Indians and beaten mercilessly — all while the devil-eyed, soulless Indians laugh maniacally at all the delicious pain they are inflicting.

The great thing about these captivity stories is that they allowed the narrator to enter an Indian village and describe the social structure and behaviour of the heathens in their natural environment. It's kind of like when you and your parents were invited to your teacher's house for dinner and the next day you get to tell your friends all about it at school; the same kind of horrors described at that dinner occur in these captivity stories.

The captivity narratives were rarely based in fact. Many of the writers simply took existing stereotypes and expanded on them to quench the reader's thirst for descriptions of Native brutality. The hero of these stories is often a white male who eventually outsmarts the brute force of the savages through his own superior physical prowess. Basically, it was the old cliché, "If I can just... free my hands... from these ropes..." But once he does, then with his superior white intellect, his mighty white fists and the divine power of the bible in his breast pocket, he easily defeats the swarm of Bad Indians in one fell swoop. The Indians aren't hard to defeat though, because Bad Indians are never organized, stab each other in the back, and are just out and out stupid — easily distracted by baubles and trinkets like an infant by car keys dangled in front of him. In the lazier captivity narratives, the white man somehow gets his hands on some rum and just throws it to the Indians, who cut each other's throats to get a taste. In captivity stories, Indians love themselves some hooch.

If it's a white woman who is captured in these narratives, then watch out! You've got yourself a bestseller, a real page-turner! These were the most popular captivity narratives because they focused on the sanctity of the most threatened and coveted of all European resources: a white woman's virginity. In Indian captivity stories, Indians love themselves some white woman.

In these narratives, the white woman is always a pious, God-fearing Christian who is repulsed, absolutely repulsed, by fierce... powerful... lean-bodied... dark-skinned men with abs of steel... chests like iron shields... and hands that could tear a garment, bustle and all, in one powerful swipe from her quivering, sweat-drenched, milky flesh. Absolutely repulsed! These narratives were written by white men long before *Cosmopolitan* and Harlequin romance turned these plots into tales of titillation. But I digress.

So long before these scenarios morphed into female erotica, they were cautionary tales of female propriety. They were the horror movies of their day in the same way that the young virgin woman is always the last one alive at the end of slasher films. In other words, young ladies were best to keep their virginity and their Christian faith intact or the Indians would get them. Ooga booga! In these tales, white women were always captured and kept alive to be used as sexual slaves for the short-haired Bad Indians. It was no wonder that Indian men craved white women though, since the Native women in these narratives were often described as inhuman, lice-covered screaming banshees with bad teeth and the sexual morals of un-spayed dogs.

In some narratives, if the captive woman is especially pious she could sometimes convince a Bad Indian to set her free before she was tainted by the savages. The Indian would oblige and be promptly killed by his own. No matter though, he would gladly die knowing that he preserved the purity of the angelic white woman. Unfortunately though, in most captivity novels the white women were ferociously raped, degraded and humiliated by the wicked Indians. When the woman is eventually rescued by the white hero, she is eternally grateful to be liberated from these red devils and she reveals that the only thing that kept her alive was her Christian faith and the belief that white justice would inevitably prevail over the evil-doers. The End. Quite a gripping yarn, huh? Now here's what *actually* happened back then...

Yes, it is absolutely true that Native people did take captives even before the white man arrived. The Haida on the west coast of Canada had a history of capturing other Natives up and down the coastline and forcing them into slavery. The Cherokee in the US also kept black slaves at the same time as southern plantation owners. There are also many accounts of the Iroquois torturing whites and forcing them to run gauntlets where they would be clubbed and beaten. It's up for interpretation whether this treatment was in retaliation for centuries of broken treaties, forced relocation, stolen lands, poverty-stricken conditions, disease and imposed religion, or — if the Iroquois were just mean. I mean, the Iroquois did sport versions of the short-haired mohawk hairdo, so, you know...

The reality of many of the real, live captivity stories is that captives were often integrated into the Native tribe. Children were adopted to replace Native children who had passed away and were raised by the Indians as their own. The adult men and women were assimilated and treated as equals. The adopted white men sat on tribal councils, married within the tribe, participated in ceremonies and had a voice in tribal decisions as if they had been born Indian. The same went for the women who, in the majority of tribes, held very respected and honoured places in Native society. Quite often the women's council was the last word in the major decision-making process. Native tribes frequently governed by consensus and that included honouring the point of view and opinions of everyone in the community from elders to men to children to women. This was shocking for many white women who had come from societies where they were considered the property of their husbands, were not allowed to vote and were forbidden from doing practically anything that white men could do. In a sense, being taken captive by the Indians was often a liberating experience for white women.

61

Many of the captivity narratives were based on actual events but more often than not they were fictionalized to satisfy the public's fascination with Indian savagery. This is not to say that the high frequency of kidnapping was fictionalized. In New England alone, the century between King Philip's War and the end of the French and Indian Wars in 1763 saw almost 1,700 New Englanders taken captive. During the Indian Wars between whites and Plains Indians throughout the 1800s, hundreds of women and children were captured. The number of real-life captives ensured there was no limit of captivity stories to suit every taste.

The most negative portrayals of Indian captivity were written by the Puritans, who used the narratives as cautionary tales regarding the sanctity of the Puritan soul. In these stories, captivity by

Indians was a test from God and only through steadfast faith and unwavering devotion could the Puritan hope to find God's redemption. One of the most popular captivity memoirs of all time was *A Narrative of the Captivity and Restoration of Mrs. Mary Rowlandson*, written in 1682 by Mary Rowlandson — kind of. Following her real-life captivity, Mary Rowlandson returned to her fellow Puritans and her accounts were interpreted and written down by the white men of her community. Since Puritan men already had a negative opinion about Native cultures, it is likely that Rowlandson's narrative as well as many similar narratives were "massaged" to further a religious and social agenda. This is not to say that many of the women who were held captive enjoyed their time as prisoners; however, methinks these narratives doth protest too much.

Historians have disregarded the captivity narratives due to their one-sided, Eurocentric ideologies. Scholars who are knowledgeable about real-life Native societies tend not to view captivity narratives as factual glimpses into Native culture but rather as value-laden judgments or religious propaganda. In most cases, though, the captivity narrative is mostly studied as an example of how white society constructed the Indian as the "other." Unfortunately, captivity novels are often mistakenly regarded as factual accounts of life amongst the Indians, even to this day.

There are numerous accounts in which white captives preferred and adopted the lifestyle of their Native captors. During numerous prisoner exchanges, white captives often had to be torn kicking and screaming from their adoptive Native families. Children who had been raised by Indian families were frequently traumatized when they were taken from their Native communities and forced to reintegrate into the dominant culture. Many adult and young captives who assimilated chose to stay with their Indian families and never returned to live in mainstream society.

One famous example is Mary Jemison, who was captured as a young girl in 1755 and chose to live with the Seneca for the rest of her life. (By the way, were all women named Mary back then? Just wondering.)

The captivity story was such a large part of early American literature that when the Hollywood western rolled around, screenwriters basically recycled all the themes and formulas and put them on the screen as a continuing ode to the brave frontiersmen. By that time, literature had embedded such a negative perception of Native people that the Hollywood western was often perceived as a factual, documentary-like depiction of Native people in the Old West. Unfortunately, the Hollywood western is also where a lot of people get their education about Native people. Okay, so when First Nations people were not murdering white men and violating white women, what did they like to do to unwind? What did they... oh, I don't know... like to eat?

63

Man-eating Eskimos

In 1854, the explorer-physician John Rae wrote a report published by *The Times of London* that "Eskimos" had found the remains of the lost Franklin expedition. According to the Eskimos the corpses of the Franklin expedition appeared to have been cannibalized by members of their own party. Franklin's widow and other surviving relatives refused to accept this version and accused the Eskimos who had made the discovery of being liars. An editorial in *The Times* also demanded a further investigation: "Is the story told by the Esquimaux the true one? Like all savages they are liars, and certainly would not scruple at the utterance of any falsehood, which might, in their opinion, shield them from the vengeance of the white man." National literary treasure Charles Dickens echoed the sentiments of *The Times* and English society at that time when he wrote in his weekly magazine, "We believe every savage to be in his heart covetous, treacherous, and cruel."

Dr. Rae, on the other hand, had lived among the Inuit and described them as "a bright example to the most civilized people." In contrast, he described the crew of the Franklin party as "undisciplined" and suggested they were poorly treated and "would have mutinied under privation." Naturally, Rae's "savage-loving" attitude destroyed his career, and attempts by Lady Franklin and Charles Dickens to glorify the memory of the Franklin party resulted in Rae being shunned by the British establishment. Modern historians have since confirmed that Rae discovered the Northwest Passage and have also verified the Eskimo reports that when the Franklin crew said they were going to have a friend for dinner they literally had a friend for dinner.

64

These are just a few of the countless examples of how the Bad Indian image served the purposes of white ambition in the early days of North American settlement. The real proof of their effectiveness is how, even today, a Native person's co-operation and assimilation into white society will invariably earn him the label "Good Indian"—while those "Bad Indians" on the fringes of white society are still feared for their capacity to metaphorically devour Caucasians, the other white meat.

Pan-Indianism

Once the push for westward expansion had run through its most dramatic conflicts and Native people were moved onto reserves in Canada and the US, there still remained the issue of what to do with the "Indian Problem" (the official term in government documents and memos). Thus began attempts to squeeze out the last remaining evidence of Native identity under the guise of assimilation. Native culture and religion was outlawed. Indian agents were placed in charge of reserves and regulated every aspect of reserve life, ensuring that Natives rarely left the reserves. From my perspective, preventing Native people from assimilating was a strange way to get them to assimilate, but that's what the government said it was doing, so what do I know?

At this time, the idea that Indians were children who required full control by the Great White Father shifted from commonly held sentiment to official government policy. Enter the Indian residential schools, where thousands of Native children were taken from their communities and families and placed in church-run schools. The intent of the schools was to remove any last trace of their language and culture, or as Duncan Scott, deputy superintendent of Indian Affairs, wrote, "to kill the Indian in the child."

65

For the most part, the schools offered a substandard education that focused on nothing more than training the boys and girls for a life of manual and domestic labour. In addition, the schools were rife with sexual abuse, physical abuse and mental torture at the hands of the priests and nuns in charge. In many cases when pedophilia was uncovered, the offending priest or nun would simply be transferred to another residential school where the abuses would start all over again.

As a result, generations of Native people turned to alcohol, drugs and violence. Social problems exploded. Having almost wiped out the Natives' connection to their culture, language and traditional lands, the dominant culture became nostalgic for the unspoiled, untouched, noble Indians of yesteryear. Even though practically all the resources of the Canadian and US governments went toward eradicating the visibility of Native people from the continent, the symbol of the stoic and noble Indian of centuries ago remained popular to advertise products and concepts that consumers would identify as uniquely North American. Products like Land O' Lakes Butter, Indian Motorcycles and almost every holistic item on the market used Native images to advertise earthiness, all natural ingredients and made-in-America reliability.

The most significant result of the de-identification process of Native people was the amalgamation of cultures. This established a new culture known as Pan-Indianism, which is essentially the mixing together of different Native cultures in order to arrive at one all-encompassing Indian. This is why you often see movies where a tribe is wearing the wrong ceremonial wardrobe for their people or are practising traditions that didn't exist in their culture. It's not uncommon for Native actors to show up on film sets and be asked by the director to say something "in Indian." Pan-Indianism is also why modern-day Natives and non-Natives will adopt looks pieced together from a number of different cultures, i.e. beaded hair clips in an Iroquois design, Southwest turquoise jewellery, Plains-style choker, etc. — a walking smorgasbord of Native accoutrements, or a Native-jewellery Christmas tree if you will.

As Native lands were compressed and Natives of differing groups were pushed together, the idea of one Native culture became common in the documentation of Native peoples. The most prolific of these early documenters was Edward Curtis. Curtis was famous for his photographs of turn-of-the-century Native culture but he was also criticized for staging his subjects. At the turn of the twentieth century as Native rights were being denied and treaties ignored, many Natives were still able to successfully adapt to Western society. By reinforcing the images of the vanishing noble savage, many believe that Curtis undermined the very real plight of Native Americans that he was witnessing first-hand on reservations.

Curtis was famous for capturing Native people in their natural environments, but he was also known to remove all traces of Western culture from his photos despite the fact that his Native subjects might have embraced the clothing, technology or modern conveniences of the time. He frequently dressed his Native subjects in costumes that were culturally inaccurate or staged scenes and ceremonies that were not indigenous to the people he was photographing. While Curtis's motives were generally well intentioned, his manipulation of his subjects belies a commonly held belief that still exists today: that Natives of yesteryear were the real Indians and Natives adapting to the modern world are the vanishing Indians.

Indianthusiasts

This fixation on Indians of the past can be found in many European countries such as Germany, Italy and the Czech Republic, where groups of weekend warriors known as "Indianthusiasts" or "Indian hobbyists" gather in the woods over a number of days and become Indians. These hobbyists dress in buckskin outfits, live in teepees, and drum and dance and sing in the tradition of Native people or more specifically, Native people from centuries past. Many of these Indianthusiasts are so committed to upholding the past that they will often snub modern-day Natives for not being "real Indians" anymore—especially when they come to North America and cannot find the teepees, buckskin clothing and war bonnets that they are used to seeing on their European Indians back home. Despite most Natives' eye-rolling at these so-called "wannabes," it has been stated by some Native people that have spent time amongst the hobbyists that they wish North Americans had as much respect for Native people and culture. Regardless, it is still cool to hear Native languages spoken with German accents—as if Rez accents weren't thick enough!

This European fascination with "Good Indians" originated from the novels of Karl May and his popular character Winnetou, who was a German man who came to live among the Indians and became an über-Indian. Yep, that theme again. These Karl May novels were the Harry Potter books of their day and were romanticized by German people of all generations. Some of the German boys who were huge fans of Winnetou were none other than Adolf Hitler and members of his Nazi Party.

Fascist, Communist and Separatist Indians

To further add to the list of reasons why Nazis were crazy, try this one on for size. Even though the Nazis classified Native Americans among the inferior races, they still considered them to be honorary Aryans because, like the Nordic races, they also originated from the lost city of Atlantis and used the swastika as a cultural symbol. Um... WTF!?

This cuckoo theory was further propagated in the German westerns of the early twentieth century, especially in the writings of Karl May. May wrote specifically about the American West and particularly Native American culture even though he had never visited America until after most of his novels were published — and even then never made it past New York State. Nevertheless, the novels became hugely popular and influenced European perceptions of Native Americans through highly sympathetic and romanticized depictions. Like most German boys, Hitler was a huge fan of Karl May westerns and confessed that whenever he was in a tight spot he would turn to those stories and ask, "What would the Indians do?" Short answer, Hitler: not what you did!

At the beginning of the Second World War, Nazi propagandists declared that if they won the war, Germany would return huge swaths of land to the Indians. Joseph Goebbels mistakenly thought that Native Americans would be antagonistic toward America and would easily be swayed into fighting for the Nazi cause from within America. In reality, Native people had some of the highest voluntary enlistment rates per capita in most of the major wars. On the bright side, the Nazis finally got to see real-life Indians, but it was usually while staring down the barrel of an Indian's gun.

It wasn't just the Nazis who used the noble savage as a metaphor for their own struggle. With the spread of communism, a different type of cowboy and Indian movie emerged that was a lot more sympathetic to the Natives than the Hollywood western. In these communist movies, the pioneers were portrayed as the savages: imperialistic invaders with no regard for the original inhabitants of the land. To this day, many so-called "oppressed" cultures still liken their struggle to that of the Natives of the Old West. Great, so happy we can provide you with a metaphor, folks.

69

Back at home, during numerous debates in which Quebec has threatened to secede from Canada, questions have been raised about the loyalties of Quebec Natives. Quebec politicians have assumed that since Native people are constantly at odds with Canada over their sovereign status, that they would obviously side with Quebec and join them in their separation — to which the majority of Native people in Quebec have responded, "Whoa, whoa, whoa... We're going where? No, no, no, you guys can leave if you want, but this is our house. Just make sure you clean up your room before you go."

Sports Mascots

The stereotype of the ferocious, defiant Indian is at the heart of the controversy over sports mascots and whether these Pan-Indian representations honour Native people or are offensive misrepresentations. On a personal note, I've never believed that

Native American mascots were *intended* to offend Native people. I think it is fair to say that fans imbue a sports team with the qualities that represent the ideals they wish to cheer for. That is why I believe that the people that fight to keep images of the Washington Redskins, the Chicago Blackhawks or even Chief Wahoo of the Cleveland Indians (although this one is debatable) truly believe that they are honouring the fighting warrior spirit of the Natives of yesteryear — or they just have a nostalgic attachment to the team and mascots regardless of the racial or political connotations. Having said that, there are significant problems with the notion that Indian sports mascots are honouring Native people and "Indians should just get over it." Here are just a few of the arguments that pretty much every Native person endures, whenever the subject of Indian sports mascots come up.

These mascots have been around for ages, why do Indians have a problem with them now?

Well, most of these mascots and names were established before Native people had a significant voice in the dominant culture. As Native people have become more integrated and politically active, they are now expressing their concerns over what they feel are the continuing effects of colonization. That doesn't mean Natives weren't offended before, they're just more vocal about it now. Just because these mascots have been around for a long time doesn't mean they're okay. Hell, Vegemite has been around for a long time and that stuff is very much the opposite of okay.

But they're not offensive representations. They're proud, noble, stoic warrior images of Native Americans.

They're clichés. Not only that, but they are clichés based on a very narrow view of what non-Natives *want* an Indian to be. The images on those sports jerseys are what non-Natives have decided a "real Indian" looks like and are usually based on the idea of how Native people were before they became a "vanished people."

So what are we supposed to do? Have a modern-day Indian holding a whisky bottle and working in a casino?

Those are our only options!? Actually, in the view of many non-Natives these *are* the only two options. To them, there are two types of Indians: the stereotypical "Good Indian" found on their jerseys or the stereotypical "Bad Indian," which is what they believe Indians have become.

71

But we're honouring you.

Here's the thing. Native people are human beings, which means we have wildly differing opinions on all matters. There is not one Pan-Indian opinion on the subject of Indian sports mascots. Some Natives view the mascots as the second coming of smallpox, some Natives couldn't care less and some Natives think the mascots are the greatest thing since sliced fry bread. It's all a matter of opinion.

What is *not* a matter of opinion is how extreme the resistance is to Natives who voice concerns about these mascots. I guarantee you that the extreme anger and disregard for Native people on this matter would not occur if it were any other race of people on this continent voicing similar concerns. If the managers and fans of these teams were really honouring Native people, they might step back and say, "Hmmm, there are a large number of Native people who are offended by our team name and mascot. Our intent was to honour them, not offend them. Maybe we should sit down and hear their concerns and try to work out an understanding with them so we can continue to honour them in a mutually accepted way."

That doesn't happen. Instead, the reaction is often, "F**k those

Indians! They're too sensitive! They don't know what they're talking about! They should get over it! They should shut up and get a job and quit drinking and quit being a burden on society! I mean, c'mon... can't they see we honour them?"

When Native people explain from a first-hand cultural perspective why they find the mascots offensive, and they are bombarded with reasons why their opinion is wrong, why they don't have a right to be offended and why they just don't get it, that's not honouring, that's disregarding. These responses smack of the same paternalistic attitude that Native people have dealt with for centuries, in which we are regarded as children and require non-Natives to explain difficult concepts to us, including what we should think, how we should behave and especially, when we should just shut up and get over it.

Finally, go to any game where a team has a Native mascot and watch how the fans of that team "honour" Native Americans by dressing in cartoonish headdresses, buckskin and war paint. Watch how culturally aware they are when they do their offensive war whoops, make tomahawk chops and urge their team to scalp its opponents. Read the signs written in the "pigeon-Injun" broken English, that use words like "ugh," "squaw," "firewater" and other representations of Native people as inarticulate idiots, and try to remember it's all in good fun. Then try to imagine any other cultural or religious group, i.e. Jews, Asians, blacks, Latinos, Muslims, Christians, etc., for which these sort of depictions would not be shut down immediately!

But what about Notre Dame? They have the Fighting Irish mascot and you don't hear Irish people complaining.

This is the most overused of all the arguments. First of all, back when Notre Dame was considering adopting the Fighting Irish name, the university actually was concerned about the negative stereotype of the Irish as uneducated, drunken brawlers. Legend has it that the name Fighting Irish was not chosen as a slur but as a reference to the "Irish Brigades" of the Civil War who were known for their courage, ferocity and toughness in battle.

Notre Dame was the preeminent Catholic university in America at a time when Catholic was associated with Irish. As a result, Notre Dame was supported and embraced by the Irish American community. The president of the university was very sensitive to Irish opinion and input, so the Fighting Irish name would not have been adopted had it not been for the approval **73** and support of the Irish American community. In other words, the Irish chose how they wanted to be depicted and had full control over their representation. By contrast, the majority of Native American names and mascots were chosen without support, consultation or regard for the Native American community. And now that some Natives are attempting to have a say in their representation, the sports teams and fans have very little interest in their opinions — unlike the founders of Notre Dame University.

For the record, there have been some Irish people who have expressed concerns about the Fighting Irish mascot, but it has not been as widespread as Native concerns over our mascots. I guarantee that if the Irish American communities caused as much of a furor over the Notre Dame mascot, there would at least be a conversation with them over their concerns.

Only a small minority of Native people think the names and mascots are offensive.

Well no. When it *was* just a small group of Natives expressing concerns, it was easy to dismiss this as a fringe movement. However in the last few decades numerous sports writers have agreed that the depictions are offensive. Recently, veteran sports commentator Bob Costas went on national television and urged the Washington Redskins to change their name. And if that wasn't an authoritative enough voice, the President of the United States, Barack Obama, recently stated that he thought the Redskins name was offensive and should be changed. The frickin President of the United States! And he lives in Washington!!

Nevertheless, the fact that sports managers and fans still feel they do not have to be concerned about the outrage from Native protesters further proves the mainstream attitude that Natives are childish and don't know what's good for them. This patriarchal attitude is evidenced in the commonly uttered statement:

Get a Sense of Humour, Indians!

When I was eight years old, my stepfather took my mother and me on a trip to jolly ol' England. The family we were staying with had a son who owned an extensive collection of British comic books. One of the comics was a popular digest called *Beano*, which was kind of the British equivalent to *Archie*. You know, the ones that threw in Josie and the Pussycats and Little Dot and other characters that you quickly flipped past to see what Jughead was going to eat next.

As I was flipping through *Beano* I came across a comic strip called "Little Plum, Your Redskin Chum" about a young "red Indian" who belonged to the "Smellyfeet Tribe." Yeah, I know, stay with me. The members of the Smellyfeet Tribe were, of course, Plains Indians who lived in teepees, wore buckskin, spoke in broken English and had wives who were called "squaws." None of this was particularly odd to me because even in North America these representations were par for the course. However, the thing that made me suspect that these English cartoonists had not done any research into Native culture was that this Plains tribe of nomadic Indians were surrounded by totem poles.

Anybody who grew up in western Canada like I did has seen their fair share of totem poles. We all knew that totem poles were carved and raised by west coast Natives who were non-nomadic so could afford the months it took to carve a massive totem pole and raise it to stand for generations to come. Also, these totem poles can reach up to seventy feet tall, making them as stationary as you can get. The notion that the Smellyfeet Tribe could spend months carving and raising these stationary poles and then drag them to their next camp while they followed the buffalo herds was absolutely ridiculous. Perhaps this is why none of us have ever heard of the Smellyfeet Tribe — their ambition and lack of practical planning most likely led to their extinction. Fare thee well, Smellyfeet Tribe, you shall not be forgotten.

Now, I know what you're thinking: "Chill dude, it's a kid's cartoon. It's not meant to be anthropologically accurate. It's supposed to entertain and make you laugh." Which is exactly why I bring up this little cartoon from across the pond. It illustrates (see what I did there?) how Native culture, at home and around the world, is perceived as a remnant of the past and regarded as a curiosity to entertain and make you laugh. Throughout history, Native people have been called a "vanishing race," which has led to a modern-day perception that surviving Natives are the last remnants of a culture that is more or less extinct. Consequently, Native people are one of the few cultures where a representation like the Smellyfeet Tribe will elicit the response, "Get a sense of humour — it's not meant to represent real Native people." The problem is, representations like the Smellyfeet Tribe have actually come to be a commonly accepted depiction of present-day Natives.

Quite often, you will hear non-Natives say, "I'm [insert racial background here] and we make fun of ourselves all the time. Get a sense of humour!" Actually, Native communities are well known for constant laughter and an ever-present sense of humour. We make fun of ourselves and highlight our stereotypes more than anybody else, if that's even possible. So getting a sense of humour is not the problem. When people state they are Jewish, black, Latino, Irish, etc. and they make fun of themselves so why can't Natives, the difference is that when another culture steps over the line and portrays one of these groups in a negative light, they have a powerful thing going for them: consequence.

Every other culture in North America is perceived as viable and consequential in present-day society. If a certain race is offended, there will inevitably be a fear of a backlash and a corresponding conversation to remedy the situation. For some reason though, Native people are not regarded as people whose cultural concerns need to be fostered — well, Natives and the Amish. Since the common perception is that "real Indians" are extinct, then it is generally accepted that Native culture, icons, religious beliefs and traditional dress are wide open for appropriation and mocking without any fear of consequence. It's kind of like not worrying about poking an alligator because its dinosaur ancestors are dead, and then being surprised when the alligator tries to tear your arm off. "Relax alligator! Get a sense of humour!"

Every so often you will hear about fashion designers who dress their models in sexy buckskin and faux headdresses and claim they are honouring the proud history of the first inhabitants. The internet will light up with Native groups claiming the depiction is offensive, which is followed by even more responses from non-Natives that Indians should relax and get over it. Some internet posters will even claim they are Scottish and say, "What's next? Do we ban people from using kilts and tartans?" The comments inevitably lead to more racist statements like "they aren't even real Indians anymore and they should spend more time worrying about their corrupt chiefs and drinking and cleaning up their yards," etc.

Let me add this perspective: even if the offence taken by these

Native appropriations comes from a few "militant" Natives, the overwhelming response that Native people do not have a right to be concerned with these images is where most of the frustration lies with Native groups. Once a dominant society imposes what a group has the right to be offended by, they will inevitably determine which legal rights, historical agreements and even names the indigenous group should live by. When attitudes like these are directed at Native people, it can feel like North America still regards us as children in need of the guidance of Indian agents because we just... don't... get it! And after all we've done for this continent, too. Sheesh. Okay, in the words of Forrest Gump: **77** "That's all I have to say about that." Now that we have explored some of the misrepresentations that plague Native folks, let's look at some of the physical criteria society has placed on Native people to determine if one looks like a "real Indian."

Cheekbones

According to mainstream society, the most prominent designator of Native people is high cheekbones. It's such a widely accepted signifier of Native blood that many people with high cheekbones just assume they are Native. For example, Massachusetts Senator Elizabeth Warren claimed during her first campaign that she had Native American blood because a relative pointed out her grandfather had "high cheekbones like all the Indians do." The Democratic candidate ran into trouble when Harvard revealed that in the 1980s and 90s she described herself as a Native American minority in law school directories. Warren denied that she self-identified as a Native American in order to increase her chances of being hired by law firms looking to hire minorities. In order to deflect "Cheekbone-gate," Warren's handlers magically discovered that her great-great-

great grandmother was—you guessed it—Cherokee, which would make Elizabeth Warren 1/32nd Indian. Well carry on then, my Abo sista'. This example once again proves the old adage, "Cheekbones—priceless."

In the Greg Albert instructional book *Basic Drawing Techniques*, it says, "Some races of people on average have higher cheekbones than others. Native American facial structure is typically of a very pronounced brow and arch of the nose, high cheekbones and a lean, square chin." Wow, now that's specific! High cheekbones are often considered a sign of beauty and are very common amongst top models, which is why I have always said, "Nobody can be that good-looking without having some Native blood." I know there is no scientific proof to back up this statement, but I'm comfortable with spreading this stereotype.

No Body Hair

Growing up on the Rez, one of my stepfathers (that sounded awful—sorry Mom) would sit on the couch with a mirror and a pair of tweezers and pluck his miniscule hairs. He would call this act "Indian shaving." I've noticed that most of my people—the Secwepemc—are not known for our ability to grow hair on our face, chests, legs and arms. This seems to be a straight-across-the-board stereotype for Native people and has even been inflated to suggest that Native people do not grow hair in their loincloth areas, as well.

A number of years ago, a friend of mine was acting in a Canadian TV movie as a true-life Native girl who was murdered and left for dead in the cold Canadian winter. There were many scenes of the girl's body in the snow and they were filming on location in northern Canada, so a replica of my friend's body was constructed for the filming of the winter scenes. When my friend inspected her body double she noticed it was an accurate representation save for one detail: the body did not have any pubic hair. When my friend inquired where the pubic hair was, the person who designed the body double explained — to a large group of Native onlookers — that Native people did not have pubic hair. (I assume the Native onlookers immediately made appointments with their doctors to find out what those hair-like growths were down there.)

Our supposed inability to grow hair is associated with our primitive Asian ancestry, who are also stereotyped as being hairless. In fact, it is often suggested that most of the stereotypes that affect Asian people on a genetic level were carried over from Siberia and manifest themselves in the genetic makeup of Native people as well. (Yeah, that theory. Don't worry, I'll get to it.) From as far back as the 1600s, Europeans have written that Native Americans were able to grow facial hair to varying degrees, but often removed it as soon as possible because they considered excess body hair unattractive, as pointed out in William Wood's text from 1634, *New England's Prospect*:

> You cannot woo them to wear it on their chins, where it no sooner grows but it is stubbed up by the roots, for they count it as an unuseful, cumbersome, and opprobrious excrement, insomuch as they call him an Englishman's bastard that hath but the appearance of a beard...

While it is difficult to determine whether or not pre-contact Natives allowed their body hair to grow wilder than a hippie girl at a folk festival, it would appear that after contact the removal of whatever body hair Natives had was more of a negative reaction to looking like or being associated with Europeans. Ouch, harsh. So while there really isn't definitive scientific evidence that Natives are less able to grow body and facial hair, we Natives do know that there is definitely a phenomenon known as "Indian beard." Don't ask to see one, it's just sad.

Lean Bodies

Part of the mystique of Native people, which greatly led to the perception of Native people as savages, was the image of Natives wearing very little clothing. All descriptions from the time of contact to the turn of the last century describe Native people as being athletic with hard bodies and exceptional health. Hey, if I could describe my somewhat flabby body that way, I might walk around in nothing but a loincloth too, stereotypes be damned. So, while the image we see of the rippling-muscled warrior or lean Indian maiden of yesteryear might have held some truth, the reality today is that Native people are more likely to be overweight and suffering from diabetes and heart disease, which have reached almost epidemic levels in Native communities.

The reason for the dramatic shift can be easily linked to two major changes in traditional diet and traditional lifestyle. Go to any Indian gathering and the foods are bound to be the same across North America. If they are lucky enough to have wild meat, i.e. deer, salmon, moose, then that is a real score. Wild berries and rice are also found at traditional gatherings. Unfortunately, what generally passes as traditional Indian food these days is actually a diet introduced by Europeans and has been adopted by Native people as a result of poverty and relocation from sustenance-rich lands. Items like fry bread or bannock are prime examples of foods that are considered Indian but were actually introduced by voyageurs and colonists as bread that did not require leavening and could be cooked over a fire. As Natives had more contact with Europeans, they began to adopt and share different foods from their respective cultures. Unfortunately, the Europeans introduced items like white flour, white sugar, and items high in sugar and starch. This was a shock to many Native diets that were used to seasonal foods like fresh fruits, vegetables and wild game.

As Native people were removed from their land and placed on reserves, they were often forced to survive off government commodities such as flour, sugar, cheese or other foods that could be stored for long periods of time since they were often not allowed to leave the reserve to hunt or fish. Often the lands they were moved onto were fallow and unable to grow anything substantial. Today, in the more remote areas, Natives have to contend with a lack of fresh fruits and vegetables, as transporting them is difficult and very costly. Due to their surroundings and poverty, inexpensive frozen, canned and processed foods are sometimes the only options. This is a common problem in many poverty-stricken areas across North America, but unlike areas where one can take public transportation to a grocery store, many Native communities do not have access to transportation, and in some fly-in communities they don't even have access to roads.

As a result, diabetes and related health problems have reached epidemic proportions in Native communities. Interestingly, there has been a new movement of Native people that have gone back to eating only traditional foods and in the seasonal manner of their ancestors. The resulting weight loss and reverse of health problems has been dramatic. As mentioned, though, in many communities the ability to eat in a traditional way is hampered by the fact that so much damage to the traditional way of life has occurred that the land of their ancestors is practically non-existent. Also, with the advent of genetically modified foods, even the traditional foods that were indigenous to North America have become so processed that much of the original nutrition has been altered out of them. So even though many Native people will say they are dedicated meat eaters just like their ancestors, I can't say I have ever seen a petroglyph drawing of an Indian hunter chasing down a wild Big Mac.

Clothing

I've done a number of plays, films and TV shows where I played a "Native"—which is convenient because I have been researching that role my entire life. Whenever I am playing a modern-day Native I can already guess what the costume is going to be before I even attend the costume-fitting. Everything will have been bought at the bargain bin of Kmart or the Salvation Army—usually a lot of old denim or plaid work shirts. There is definitely a Native uniform in the minds of mainstream North Americans—either a western motif or a slovenly dressed poor person.

Traditionally, Native people dressed for practicality but they also took pride in their appearance and were frequently decorated. Indians were rarely plain-looking. They dressed and sought to look their best. It has been documented ad nauseam that one of the reasons Native people were so susceptible to disease was because they were notoriously clean and bathed daily as part of ceremony. This was the complete opposite of Europeans who came from filthy conditions in Europe and rarely bathed. Even today Natives have many ceremonies and traditions that revolve around proper grooming, especially of hair, which is still considered a very sacred part of the body and is treated with great care and respect.

In addition, when Native people came into contact with Europeans, they incorporated a lot of European clothing into their own traditional dress. They not only heightened the use of European decorations such as glass, plastic beads and coloured threads, but they also created entire artistic cultures out of the use of these European items. It is interesting that the idea of dressing to enhance oneself in fineries has become considered as a white trait and is shunned by many Natives.

Nowadays, clothing has become one of the most commonly appropriated cultural items. The wearing of feathers, jewellery or Native designs is an oft-commodified practice by Native and non-Natives alike. It is not uncommon for people to claim a Native heritage no matter how tenuous, and then proceed to dress head to toe in every variation of Pan-Indian decoration they can find as proof of their Native heritage.

83

Indians of Today

For the most part, Indians of today are regarded as the bad guys again — at least in the mainstream media. Every day in areas where there is a sizeable Native population, the media paints Native people and their claims of sovereignty as contrary to progress and a drain to taxpaying North Americans. The image once again is of the drunken Indian or the Indian looking for a handout, not just on the street but from the government. With over fifty percent of all Natives in Canada living in urban centres, that image is pushed constantly as we hear more and more about Native homelessness, alcoholism, lack of education and violence.

Since North Americans have more Native people living amongst them, they are more likely to witness the small percentage of Native people that are drunk or homeless and associate that image with the greater majority of Native people. Propaganda over centuries has served itself well, and the ongoing stereotype of Native people as either "Good Indians" or "Bad Indians" has been quite effective in convincing North Americans that complete assimilation is the only way to solve the persistent Indian Problem. If this is the belief you cling to, then you are going to hate reading the upcoming chapters. Enjoy...

NATIVES & ALCOHOL

"Why the only Indian on *Cheers* was a wooden Indian"

SITUATED IN THE PICTURESQUE MOUNTAINS OF THE Canadian Rockies stands an amazing cultural institution known as the Banff Centre. It is a haven for artists of all disciplines, all races and all walks of life. The Banff Centre is considered by many to be the Canadian artistic equivalent of Shangri-La. When I was in my twenties I was invited there on numerous occasions to participate in script readings, acting workshops or whatever artistic discipline I stumbled my way through back then. I was mostly invited under the umbrella of the Native Arts program, which focused mainly on the development of... well, Native Arts (I guess some things don't require explanation).

The program provided the best training for Native artists and its mandates were ahead of its time. But there was one aspect of the Native Arts program that was not ahead of its time; in fact, it was downright primitive. Before any Native artists could participate in the programs we were required to sign a form stating that we would not consume any alcohol. That meant no glass of wine with your dinner or a scotch as a nightcap, or — as I have witnessed from some elected MLAS — no whisky with your breakfast. (I'm not naming names, I'm just saying there is stuff that goes on behind the walls of parliament that would make even Ozzy Osbourne say, "C'mon guys, that's a little excessive.")

It's important to note that the Banff Centre's Native Arts program was not a religious-based program. Sure, traditional smudging ceremonies, dances and rituals were incorporated into the program where alcohol use is frowned upon; however, alcohol is not forbidden in Native religions as it is in the Muslim faith or the Mormon faith. Nope, the reason we had to sign the forms was to ensure that Indians didn't drink and start acting all... "Indian." The non-Native participants were not required to sign anything. So, after the day's artistic endeavours, we Natives would sit in the campus pub and sip our fruit juices and sodas, while the non-Native artists around us drank copious amounts of alcohol and, in many cases, started acting all... "Indian." For the record, the *No Drinking for Indians* policy at the Banff Centre was scrapped quite a while ago and so far the Banff Centre has not been burned to the ground with a barrage of flaming arrows. Way to keep it together, Indians!

A lot of people will hear about this policy and think, "Yeah that makes sense." Even if the sentiment does not come from a place of racism, there is still the notion that Native people would probably be wise not to drink anyway, considering their genetic predisposition to alcoholism, their genetic lack of tolerance to alcohol and their genetic heredity of alcoholics. And that's just Indians who are saying these things. Based on personal experience I would say there are just as many Native people as non-Natives

85

who believe we are born alcoholics due to our history and genetic make-up. In other words, Native people are born into "original sin"—or "original sauce," if you will.

It's not only Natives who cite predisposition as an excuse for multiple trips to the beer fridge. You hear people from all backgrounds claim, "Of course I drink, I'm [choose one of the following: Irish, Russian, Australian, French, a writer, a cop, a soldier, a Hobbit, the Man on the Grassy Knoll...]." There seems to be no end to the reasons that one is culturally or genetically predisposed to drinking. However, what seems to separate those drinking cultures from that of the Native persuasion is the stereotype that Natives drink too much, they can't hold their liquor and they are all just "bad drunks."

Even the Irish, who suffer from the same stereotype as Natives for their penchant for drink, have a yearly holiday called St. Patrick's Day that celebrates not just Irish culture but Irish drinking—the suggestion being that Irish culture and Irish drinking are one and the same. The result is a holiday or rather a holy day for alcoholics in which public drunkenness, fighting and vomiting in the streets is perfectly acceptable and is even downright fun! Can you imagine if Native American Heritage Day in the US or Aboriginal Day in Canada linked their cultural celebrations to alcohol because of their longstanding drinking history? What if instead of green beer on St. Patrick's Day, bars advertised redskin red wine or heathen hot toddies or Aboriginal absinthe or Metis mai tais (I could spend all day coming up with these). It would never happen, because in the eyes of most of the world, Natives and alcohol are never associated with the "F" words: "fun," "festive" or "feliz." Nope, Native drinking is more commonly associated with the words "tragic," "uncivilized" and "chronic"—not exactly the image you want to base a holiday around. Could you imagine a bunch of red T-shirts printed with the slogan: *Kiss me*

I'm Indian... and therefore genetically predisposed to self-destructive alcoholic behaviour! Let the good times roll!

So how did we get saddled with this unfortunate stereotype? Why is it that bartenders sigh and roll their eyes when they see an Indian approach the bar? And when that same Indian orders a non-alcoholic beverage does the bartender immediately assume the Native customer is in AA? Why is it when people walk past skid row and see one drunk Indian surrounded by ten drunk whites, they turn up their noses and say, "Look at that drunk Indian," as if the Indian is the star of some alcoholic version of *Where's Waldo?* Are we really the worst drunks in North America, or is North America just programmed to view all Native people that way? To answer these questions let's take a look at some of the most common stereotypes about Native drinking, starting with:

87

Alcohol Is New

Remember when you were in junior high and you and twelve friends shared a six-pack of beer and you all got SO WASTED? Then the next day you found out that the beer was actually non-alcoholic but you could swear the 0.5% went right to your head? This scenario is similar to what many people believe occurred during the introduction of alcohol into Native communities. The stereotype is that Native people were all natural before Europeans came, eating grass and grubs and drinking nothing but fresh glacial water, so when alcohol was introduced to the pure and delicate Native digestive system, they freaked out like Scooby Doo after a Scooby Snack. The shock of that first drink made the Indians instant alcoholics and the alcoholic gene was passed onto future generations so now when Native people drink they immediately go bat-guano crazy! Admit it, you kind of believe that... maybe a little... maybe a smidge?

The first stereotype we have to debunk is that Native people never tipped back a cold one before Europeans arrived. In places like Mexico and Central and South America, alcoholic beverages were frequently used in cultural and ceremonial practices. It was sort of like Uncle Herschel who rarely drinks except when there is a bar mitzvah where he tips back a few and dances the macarena a little too enthusiastically. First peoples of the southwestern United States would tap the saguaro cactus and drink its buzz-inducing juice in order to bring about rainfall. Since the Southwest is very dry, they often drank copiously due to their belief that the more cactus juice they drank, the more rain would fall. (Yeah, I've used that excuse before.)

There has also been evidence of a variety of fermented beers and wines found in northern areas of the continent and even in the far north amongst some Inuit tribes. Straight across the board though, Native alcohol use generally did not involve excessive drunkenness, but was controlled and supervised for use in highly ritualized occasions. It's also important to note that these early alcohols were a result of fermentation; distilled alcohol didn't really make an appearance until the Europeans arrived.

Another fallacy is that when Europeans finally introduced distilled liquor to the Natives, they immediately went bonkers. Actually, documentation of Natives' first encounters with European alcohol include no descriptions of drunkenness or debauchery, starting with a Jacques Cartier drinking session in 1545. So if Natives had a history with alcohol but not alcoholism, and early introductions to European alcohol were congenial, then where did it all go wrong? It definitely became more damaging, likely due to the alcohol content increasing, the more convenient availability compared to having to divert food supplies into the production of alcohol, and no doubt the dramatic social changes that came with exposure to European culture.

European Influences

So how profound was the switch from fermented to distilled alcohol? Let me put it this way: you know how your parents complain that weed in the 1960s was mellow and groovy but nowadays it's like a mix between crack and plutonium? The switch from fermented to distilled was as much of a buzz kill in Native communities.

When the Spanish arrived in the Americas, they quickly set up their own liquor-making facilities so they wouldn't have to import it, which led to greater availability of ready-made hooch. As a result, drinking became more widespread and it was harder to limit alcohol consumption to set holidays. In other words, even though the rules are pretty strict about keeping your alcohol inside the beer garden, there are always a couple jackasses who insist on walking out with their plastic cups full of Molson Golden. Well, imagine thousands of people leaving the beer garden at once and being all drunk and obnoxious around the children and families on the fairgrounds. This sort of increase in unrestrained drinking led to a dramatic spike in violence within Native communities.

In other parts of North America, the real alcohol trade did not begin its onslaught until 1650. Once the French and English colonists discovered that their sugar in the West Indies could be distilled in North America and converted into alcohol, that's when liquor became a primary tool in the fur trade. A lot of folklore surrounds the various forms of liquor traded in the West with First Nations peoples. One type of drink was basically just alcohol mixed with ginger, molasses and red pepper. It was then coloured with black chewing tobacco and sometimes opium, then watered down and boiled to make firewater. The word "firewater" came from the act of tossing the alcohol into the fire to see if it ignited, to then be considered a good batch. Despite what movies suggest, there is little to no evidence that the term "firewater" derived from

Indians attempting to make sense of this foul liquid by using a colourful primitive descriptor. Indians knew crappy hooch when they tasted it.

Needless to say, whether you were Native or non-Native, most of the distilled alcohol in the North American frontier was not intended to sip in a parlour with a cigar amongst gentlemen. It was meant, as modern-day Canadians might put it, "to get you hosed"—which brings me to an interesting stereotype that back in the day, Europeans were able to control their alcohol consumption and drink moderately while only the Indians drank to excess.

Twaddle and codswallop! (Or whatever the kids are saying these days.) The truth is early settlers drank a lot, drank hard and frequently drank to excess. And here's the part that really cracks me up: dating back to the times of antiquity, the northern Europeans who eventually came to settle North America had a reputation for being "bad drunks" in the eyes of southern Europeans. Doesn't feel very good, does it?

European Drinking Habits

Historians have made some interesting discoveries about drinking practices amongst pre-Columbian Europeans. It has been suggested that once Roman influence spread over Europe, certain differences in drinking patterns began to emerge. In the Mediterranean areas where it was sunny and grapes were plentiful, people began to enjoy wine with meals. However, Roman influence ensured the practice was done in moderation except during feasts and celebrations, in which they were allowed to party like it was 1999 (BC).

In northern Europe, the alcohol was grain- and honey-based and the production of these crops was susceptible to cold weather, which meant alcohol could often not be produced for several seasons. When alcohol was available, the northern Europeans would often drink to excess and suffer the common problems associated with binge-style drinking. In fact, alcohol was such a huge part of these European communities that farming communities were often established that focused mainly on the processing of alcohol.

In addition, the weather and harsh conditions frequently led to depression, and alcohol consumption became a common way for people to cope with life's challenges. Even today, in Eastern Europe where life is notoriously difficult, alcohol consumption is well above the norm both as a cultural phenomenon and as a coping mechanism. These same issues will make an encore when we examine Native people's so-called genetic predisposition as a reason for alcoholism.

91

Partying in the New World

When Europeans arrived on the shores of North America, the vast majority of them were soused to the gills morning, noon and night. There are numerous documents and letters dating back to the 1600s showing that early businessmen and political leaders were very concerned that settler drinking was hurting the Jamestown colony. The founder of Georgia, James Oglethorpe, was so afraid that rum would ruin the Peach State that he tried to ban it. Puritan leaders also tried to ban liquor, even though they were constantly imbibed as well.

The problems associated with constant binge drinking were so bad that in 1660 the Plymouth Colony court was forced to provide this description: "By drunkenness it is understood a person that either lisps or falters in his speech by reason of overmuch drink or that staggers in his going or that vomits by reason of excessive drinking, or cannot follow his calling." Or as we call it in Canada, Grey Cup Weekend.

To say colonists in early American society were enthusiastic about drinking would be a huge understatement. Modern estimates place the amount consumed by the colonists somewhere in the range of 5 to 6 gallons of pure alcohol per person every year. By comparison, alcohol consumption in the United States in 2011 was around 2.3 gallons per person. It was also estimated that there were more taverns per capita than any other kind of business in colonial North America.

Alcohol was commonplace in practically every aspect of early settler life. Businessmen would take a daily break at 11 a.m. to indulge in the "elevens," which was just a polite way of saying they tossed back a round of cocktails before lunch. Working-class folk often stopped by the tavern in the morning on the way to work and then again on the way home — oftentimes forgetting to actually go home. Liquor was served at almost all public and private social gatherings.

On Election Day, candidates would ply voters with copious amounts of alcohol in hopes they could buy votes. Even in the courts, alcohol was consumed during the trial by the attorneys, the judge and even the jury. We can only assume the executioner also drank on the job, which must have resulted in some overly messy beheadings (just try getting your front door key in the lock after a night of partying, let alone accurately swing an executioner's axe). Women drank almost as much as men, although usually more privately, and children were encouraged to drink at astoundingly early ages. How do I put this delicately? The first settlers were chronic drunks... Nope sorry, I couldn't put it delicately.

The negative connotations around alcoholism were not strong enough in the early colonial public consciousness for any widespread temperance movement to take hold. Settlers either didn't recognize that chronic drinking was undermining their society, or they just didn't care. As they say: *Denial isn't just a river in Egypt.*

Indian Temperance

Even though the colonists should have been called "co-lushes," they still believed Native communities were the ones that suffered most from the effects of alcohol. Unfortunately, they were right. Accounts from both Native and colonial settlers noted that Natives who consumed alcohol frequently drank only to become intoxicated. Violence increased within Native communities, which led to the erosion of the harmony and balance that had characterized them previously. A major pitfall of the liquor trade was the fact that young Aboriginal men were the most likely to drink to the point of intoxication. Since they were the ones who provided sustenance for their tribes, poverty became more widespread when they chose to exchange their pelts for liquor.

Over time, both Natives and colonists tried to limit the alcohol trade and many colonies even passed laws to prohibit the sale of liquor. Native people were some of the most vocal protesters and constantly pushed colonial officials to penalize traders who used alcohol to tempt young men. Native communities often organized temperance movements, many of which were based in Catholic and Protestant teachings, but the most successful anti-drinking efforts originated within Native communities and used Native spiritual practices. Despite their efforts, the liquor trade thrived because traders understood the need for most trade items would bottom out but the demand for alcohol was never-ending. Colonial officials in the US and Canada were well aware of the devastating effects of alcohol but still encouraged its use in trade with the Indians.

Throughout the twentieth century, liquor was responsible for an astonishing range of social problems in Native communities. In the US alone, Native mortality rates due to alcoholism have been estimated at between three and six times higher than that of the general US population. Homicides, suicides, fetal alcohol syndrome, exposure and accidental deaths caused by motor vehicles occurred with much greater frequency in Native communities than in the rest of the population. Despite the fact alcohol-related problems were rampant in First Nations communities, no identifiable pattern of drinking existed. This fact has been a great source of confusion for researchers and scientists who love to compartmentalize Native people into data groupings, and has also led to countless research projects that attempt to link Native alcoholism to...

94 Genetics

Since the seventeenth century, so-called scientific research has attempted to link the problems associated with Native drinking habits to a genetic trait making Natives more likely to become alcoholics. The complete lack of definitive evidence supporting this fallacy has not stopped researchers from continuing to blow through grant monies to test theories on the relationship between the physiological makeup of First Nations people and alcohol consumption. The result has been numerous research projects attempting to highlight differences or "otherness" in Native bodily processes.

There has been a lot of research pointing to an enzyme that prevents certain races from processing alcohol — thereby preventing alcoholism. It has been theorized that Native people do not possess this enzyme, so when they consume alcohol their bodies allow them to drink like it's going out of style. In fact, there are many scientific studies that suggest Natives can't do a lot of things: Natives can't process alcohol, they can't process dairy, they can't process wheat, they can't, they can't, they can't... In other words, Native people are *different* from normal people. From my perspective, as long as scientists are going to continue defining our defects, they might also want to look up a definition for the word "eugenics."

Among this research is the discovery of two genes that protect people from engaging in excessive drinking. These two genetic components are found in high numbers among those of Asian descent. The findings state that when Asians drink alcohol, their skin quickly turns red, their heart rate increases, and they experience nausea and extreme tiredness. These physiological reactions stop them from wanting to continue drinking, and protects them from abusing alcohol. This negative reaction in Asians, otherwise known as "Asian flush," is present in about a third of people from East Asian descent — predominantly in individuals of Japanese, Chinese or Korean descent. Experts believe that Natives do not have these protective genes, and as a result have higher rates of alcoholism.

95

So what causes this reaction? I'm glad you asked. When the body drinks alcohol (or ethanol), enzymes in the liver metabolize the ethanol into the toxic chemical acetaldehyde — a carcinogen that causes DNA damage and other cancer-promoting effects. The liver then metabolizes the ethanol into the harmless substance acetate. Got it? Acetaldehyde: bad. Acetate: good. People with the flushing response have a genetic deficiency that does not enable the liver to break down the nasty acetaldehyde into the harmless acetate. Therefore, thereby and henceforth, the acetaldehyde builds up in the body and causes the flushing response. Scientists say that Natives and Inuit do not possess this protective gene, so the body won't stop them from drinking. Here's the thing, though: Euro-North Americans also do not possess this gene.

Now, if you're like me, you probably thought to yourself, *Wait a second, we've been told that Native people originally came from Asia so why don't Natives also suffer from this Asian flush that prevents "overmuch drinking"?* Don't worry, the researchers have an answer for everything. Since the gene responsible for Asian flush mostly exists in people of Japanese, Chinese and Korean decent and those from Central Asia don't have it, then

Natives must be more closely related to Central Asians. Way to keep that Bering Land Bridge theory alive, boys!

The problem is, scientists disagree over which Asians have this gene. Some studies say Koreans are affected and some say Koreans are not. Some studies say the majority of Asians have the gene and some say only a third have it. Regardless, what has been proven is that Asian flush is a real thing—that's science! The suggestion that they can link the absence of the Asian flush gene to high rates of Native alcoholism—that is *not* science. Worse than that, it's yet another theory that once again paints Native people as the "other."

Think about it: the Asian flush gene is not found in Native North Americans or Inuit or North Americans without Native blood (whites, blacks, others) and it is also not present in one-third or two-thirds of the Asian population (the numbers vary depending on which study you look at). So my question is, since the gene is not present in pretty much every other race except the Chinese, Japanese and *maybe* Koreans, then shouldn't every other race be genetically susceptible to alcoholism? Unfortunately, the studies often focus on comparisons to Native North American drinking habits as if that were the gold standard for data on alcoholism. Regardless, scientists have proven that Natives do not possess this flushing gene, which must prove that alcohol affects us differently, right? I mean, we are the biggest alcoholics in North America, right? Stay with me—I'll get to that.

First of all, the idea of a genetic link in Native alcoholism has largely been debunked. Leading researchers in alcohol abuse have found that there are some specific differences, but for the most part, Native people process alcohol just like any other human being. Most research confirms that the alcohol metabolization rate in Native North Americans is the same as, or even quicker, than non-Native people. Two major biopsy studies also found that the livers of Native North Americans were similar in structure and phenotype to western Europeans, despite all claims by pseu-do-science that Native guts were somehow defective. Researchers have found only one major study to suggest that Native North Americans process alcohol slower than other races, but that study was believed to have been considerably flawed.

The other thing that is rarely mentioned in studies about Native alcoholism is that the gathering of statistical data is inherently flawed. The majority of data is gathered on reserves and due to dys-function and isolation, finding an accurate representative sample has proven challenging. Health Canada officials have admitted that they find it difficult to measure alcohol and drug use on reserves because their survey-taking is impeded by cultural differences and a lack of responses. This situation makes it very challenging to accu-rately compare Aboriginal and non-Aboriginal populations.

Instead, those who study Native alcoholism are often forced to rely on data showing why Natives get sick or die. The use of this data can be misleading when you consider high rates of illness and mortality among Native people often result from geographi-cal and social conditions that aggravate alcohol-related problems in ways not experienced in mainstream Canada. It has also been admitted that data collection on Native people in urban centres is less rigorous than on reserves. Finally, the data on Native alcohol consumption tends to lump all Natives into a Pan-Indian demo-graphic and does not take into account the difference in cultures and drinking habits of different Nations across North America. Many Nations have vastly different traditions with alcohol; for example, in the United States there have been numerous studies that suggest alcohol is more of a problem with northern tribes than in southern tribes.

Even scientists who claim heredity or genetics play a factor in alcoholism will almost always say that this is only a piece of the puzzle. Researchers are now moving away from a nature *vs*. nurture model of alcohol addiction and moving toward a nature *and* nurture model. While studies have indicated that alcoholism is a potential problem for those who come from alcoholic families, there is no definitive evidence to suggest alcoholism is specifically hereditary or genetic. Most reputable scientists are very clear that genetics play a part, but they are still unclear about *how much* of a role it plays. A successful animal model of testing has yet to be introduced that provides a definitive link between genetics and alcoholism. The best evidence that has surfaced so far is that rats and mice that have not been injected with the Asian flush gene tend to drink more alcohol. They also found that rats and mice that drink more alcohol tend to have an overinflated sense of their attractiveness the closer it gets to last call.

Since it is unclear whether there is a specific gene that predetermines susceptibility to alcohol addiction, there are many who believe that anyone and everyone is susceptible to alcoholism despite one's background, race or social standing. The one thing that seems fairly consistent is that people all over the world who live in poverty or in difficult social conditions tend to drink more, get drunk more and suffer from alcoholism more. Recent studies have also suggested that those with mental health issues also have higher incidences of alcohol and substance abuse due to a need to self-medicate. Group-based support programs like Alcoholics Anonymous will suggest heredity is a factor but also maintains that alcoholism is the one problem that knows no racial or social boundaries.

Indians and Alcohol: Stats

Even if you accept that science has not been able to provide definitive proof that Native alcoholism is linked to genetics, certainly the numbers will suggest Native people have the most alcoholics per capita of any race in North America, right? I mean, it's all over the internet so it must be true, right? Well, the numbers do back up some of what these genetic scientists have said. As it turns out, the whole Asian flush thing might have an effect on Asian cultures because statistically Asian people in North America consume the least amount of alcohol and have the least amount of reported alcoholics. "So that must mean that Natives, who don't have the Asian flush gene, must drink the most, right? Right? RIGHT!?"

I hate to burst your eugenics bubble but most studies suggest that the population that drinks the most in North America and also has the most reported alcoholics is — wait for it — CAUCASIANS! (c'mon, you had to have seen that coming). Statistics from around the world list European countries as the ones with the most alcohol consumption, specifically Eastern Bloc countries, where the majority of people identify as Caucasian. In addition, results from the 2009 National Survey on Drug Use and Health shows that Euro-North Americans report drinking the most of any other race in North America.

And here's the kicker: pretty much all the studies confirm that Native people are more likely to abstain from alcohol than white North Americans are. Caucasians, you're probably wondering why we're all here today. This is an intervention. As it turns out, this whole time you have been displaying the exact same behaviour you attribute to Indians. Ain't that a bitch?

Indians and Drinking Habits

Given the data, why do most reports claim that alcohol and substance abuse is a much larger problem in Native communities than in non-Native communities? It's not that Native people can't handle their liquor or that they drink more than white people, it's the how, the why and the where of Native drinking habits that is responsible for the high statistical problems in Native communities.

What distinguishes Native drinking from non-Native drinking is that Native people who do drink lean toward binge drinking. The definition for binge drinking is different throughout the world but it is usually classified as having five or more drinks if you're a dude or four or more drinks if you're a babe — all in one sitting. So yeah, pretty much every time you drank while on vacation in Cancun: binge drinking. Another more specific definition states that those five drinks (dudes) and four drinks (babes) must have been consumed in one sitting at least once in a two-week period for it to count as binge drinking. So I guess what this means is if you drank an entire case of beer by yourself, crashed your car and ended up in the drunk tank, but waited another three weeks before doing it again, then you're totally good. Binge drinking is also common among groups of people that are temporarily removed from their familiar surroundings or stable environments. That's why excessive binge drinking is fairly common among groups like university students, soldiers or any others placed in foreign situations for extended periods of time. That's also why having a shot of rum with breakfast would never fly back home in Moose Jaw, Saskatchewan, but seemed perfectly acceptable when you were in Barbados for two and a half weeks.

Obviously not all Native people that drink are binge drinkers. There are many who have a glass of wine at dinner and that's it, but the binge drinking model greatly explains the reason for the higher statistical problems in Native communities despite the lower statistical occurrences of alcohol consumption. And what are those statistical problems specifically? Again, I'm glad you asked.

First Nations

Alcohol-related deaths among First Nations are at least three times higher than the national average, despite the fact that alcohol use is lower among First Nations (66%) compared to the general population (79%). Among those First Nations who do drink, the percentage of heavy drinkers (16%) is double that of the general population (8%). And just like the old days, First Nations men are twice as likely to be heavy drinkers (21%) compared to women (10%).

Metis

Alcohol abuse within Metis communities is considered to be a significant problem; however, an accurate study on Metis alcohol use has yet to be provided. Since the Metis lineage derives from a mix of differing Native and European groups, it's unlikely that any genetic studies would be able to link high rates of alcoholism to race. However, the Metis do share a similar history of cultural segregation, discrimination and poverty with their First Nations brethren.

Inuit

Alcohol use in Inuit communities is substantially lower than in the rest of Canada, both Aboriginal and non-Aboriginal. However, among those Inuit who do drink, the drinking pattern once again leans toward binge drinking. In Nunavik, which comprises the northern third of Quebec, there has been a seventeen-percent increase in alcohol use since 1992. Of those Nunavik residents who do drink, ninety percent of them have reported drinking heavily within the previous year, a rate that is double that of the general population.

So what do these statistics suggest? In a nutshell, Aboriginal people as a whole drink less than non-Aboriginal North Americans but those that do imbibe tend to drink to excess. There are a lot of theories given for why Native drinking styles follow this pattern and why this pattern results in such high incidences of death, injury and violence. As Richard Thatcher states in his book *Fighting Firewater Fictions*, the binge-drinking pattern occurs largely due to a feeling of hopelessness and a lack of reward due to career trajectories, since there is limited economic potential or hope for Native inclusion in the economy of Canada.

In other cases, there is a historical link to learned behaviour of binge drinking from the Europeans who shared their liquor with Native people and frequently drank in binge-drinking style. Later, when alcohol was outlawed in Native communities, the practice was to drink as much as possible in as short a time as possible in order to avoid prosecution. However, the most common theory nowadays is that alcohol and substance abuse is linked primarily to Native people's desire to escape extremely negative social conditions. This theory is often scoffed at by people in the mainstream who have been inundated with the stereotype that Native people drink in excess not because of a defective social system but rather because Native people have a defective character. There exists an overwhelming misrepresentation that Native people live off handouts and don't have to work, so they just sit around and drink all day. This stereotype that Canadian taxpayers are paying for Natives to sit in free houses on free land and drink free alcohol completely ignores the realities of social conditions in Native communities.

Native Social Conditions

Research has found that North American Natives deal with a disproportionate amount of stress from the expectation to fully integrate into the dominant culture while also struggling with the loss of their own culture and traditions. They are also expected to integrate into the mainstream with educational and economic tools that are light years behind the dominant culture. Factor all this in with the devastating effects of residential school abuse and its intergenerational legacy and you've got yourself a Molotov cocktail (no pun intended) of deep-rooted and chronic social trauma. In these cases, alcohol is often used as a way to cope with feelings of inadequacy and lack of self-esteem due to this cultural and social trauma.

Suicide

One of the most shocking statistics in Canada is the suicide rate amongst First Nations and Inuit people. In his 2008 article "Aboriginal Mental Health: The statistical reality," published in *Visions Journal,* Saman Khan reported the suicide rate among First Nations people is twice the national average and in Inuit communities up to eleven times higher. In Nunavut, twenty-seven percent of all deaths since 1999 have been suicides, placing Nunavut as having one of the highest suicide rates in the world — especially among youth — and the number shows no signs of decreasing.

Khan also noted that in both the First Nations and Inuit communities, females attempt suicide more frequently than males, with nineteen percent of females and thirteen percent of males having attempted suicide. In the rest of Canada only about four percent of females and two percent of males have attempted suicide. However, when it comes to completed suicides, males outnumber females and the group with the highest suicide rates are youth between the ages of fifteen to twenty-four. In that age group, completed suicides among First Nations youth is five to seven times the national average.

Depression

Despite the alarmingly high rates of suicide amongst Inuit people, recorded rates of depression are far below the Canadian average. According to Statistics Canada, only three percent of Inuit reported having suffered from depression and only six percent were considered at high risk of suffering from depression. These results are puzzling considering the high rates of suicide amongst this group, but one theory suggests that data-gathering methods for the Inuit are not as accurate as they are for the rest of the Canadian population. Another explanation is that depression among the Inuit will instead take the form of problems with drugs and alcohol, violent episodes or brushes with the law. First Nations people experience major depression at twice the national average. A survey from 1997 found that of all First Nations adults living on-reserve, sixteen percent of them suffered from major depression. In the rest of Canada, only about eight percent of the population suffers from major depression.

Mental Health Treatments

Even though First Nations and Inuit people drink less alcohol than the general Canadian population, it's interesting to note that alcohol abuse is perceived as a major problem for these groups within their communities. In fact, three-quarters of all First Nations and Inuit people surveyed have claimed that they believe alcohol use is a problem in their community. About a quarter of all First Nations and Inuit people feel they have a personal problem with alcohol.

Despite the unique set of mental health challenges facing Aboriginal people, what may be surprising is that a 2002–03 survey found about seventy percent of First Nations adults living on reserves felt their physical, emotional, mental and spiritual lives were completely in balance. Now for those of you thinking that these Aboriginal people are simply in denial, research has also found that Aboriginal people experiencing mental health problems, both on- and off-reserve, were more likely than the rest of Canada to seek professional help. While only about eight percent of all non-Aboriginal Canadians suffering from mental health issues were likely to seek help, the number of Aboriginal people with mental health issues seeking help was as high as a whopping seventeen percent. It has been suggested that these numbers would probably be higher if more Aboriginal people living in isolated areas had greater access to mental health professionals.

So how do we explain the stigma that Aboriginal people are more prone to drinking and are more wacko in the head than non-Aboriginal people when the numbers don't really support that stereotype? I mean, it's statistics, right? Numbers don't lie, right? Well, numbers don't lie, but the problem with statistics is that often what the numbers claim to represent is a lie. Let me explain.

Health Canada and Statistics Canada have admitted that collecting data on Aboriginal people is extremely difficult, both on- and off-reserve, and the reliability of available statistics is extremely flawed. As we have seen, the majority of data on alcohol and drug abuse in Aboriginal communities focuses mainly on why we get sick and die. What is not made clear to Canadians is that high instances of illness and mortality due to alcohol are usually more deeply rooted in geographical and socio-economic conditions than in the actual drinking. It is nearly impossible to compare alcohol-related illness and mortality rates in Aboriginal communities to non-Aboriginal communities since the majority of Aboriginal communities contend with issues that would be unfathomable in mainstream Canada.

Most of the data surrounding alcohol-related problems in Aboriginal communities comes from first-hand accounts of those who respond to surveys. To paraphrase the first tenet of Alcoholics Anonymous, in order to deal with a problem you must first admit that one exists. As we have seen, Aboriginals are more likely to admit to problems and seek help than non-Aboriginals, which skews the statistics of alcohol-related problems in Aboriginal communities higher than non-Aboriginal communities simply because Native people are more self-aware and sensitive to issues surrounding alcohol.

In Native communities the history of dysfunction is being discussed and debated more freely, resulting in more Native communities' willingness to identify issues of mental health and alcoholism. This constant discussion about the damages of alcohol may also explain the higher-than-average rates of abstaining from alcohol as well as large-scale movements to heal our communities through traditional Native practices. More good news is that about one-third of Aboriginal people that responded to surveys believe that progress is being made in reducing alcohol and drug use in their communities.

Look, Aboriginal people might be overstating their alcohol problems or non-Aboriginal people might be understating theirs. Or alcohol might be a greater problem in Aboriginal communities than in non-Aboriginal communities. It's hard to say. The point is, the data on how bad alcohol-related problems are in Native communities is contradictory, flawed and very misleading, and unfortunately the numbers are often taken at face value and misinterpreted as statistical fact. There are numbers that do have a little more validity, and those revolve around death and mortality, but again the social challenges faced by Native people are seldom taken into account when comparing these numbers to non-Native communities.

Mortality and Injury

An unmistakable problem that does occur from binge drinking is the high rate of death, injury and violence in Native communities. The leading causes of death in Aboriginal communities are by injury and poisoning, both of which can be linked to alcohol abuse. In his study "Native Americans, Neurofeedback, and Substance Abuse Theory," Matthew J. Kelley reports that the Navajo people in the southwestern United States have suffered from alcohol-related deaths at a rate more than double that of the overall US population. However, what is often not included in this statistic is that Native and non-Native people in the southwestern US consume alcohol at a fairly even rate. Since both groups drink pretty much the same amount of alcohol, this would suggest that a number of external factors are responsible for the higher-than-average numbers of alcohol-related problems.

107

These higher mortality rates can be linked to a number of social, cultural and environmental factors, such as extreme poverty, poor nutrition and the lack of readily available medical attention. Kelley also found a large percentage of alcohol-related deaths from cold weather exposure and the difficulty of having to travel great distances in order to receive medical attention among the Navajo people. These are not just Native problems, though; they are common rural problems. In comparison, the number of alcohol-related deaths and injuries in non-Native rural counties in the Southwest are almost identical to those in Native rural communities. The only difference is, when reporting on the non-Native counties the descriptions focus more on the problems with lack of infrastructure and not on inherent problems of alcoholism, as they so often do when referring to Native alcohol use.

The problems associated with Native substance abuse are frequently aggravated by a number of economic and environmental issues such as disproportionate strain placed on limited reserve-based medical, social and criminal systems. For example, Native people who sustain mild injuries while drinking are more likely to die because they are located many hours from a hospital. Even if a person does manage to get treatment, medical facilities on reserves or in rural areas may be ill-equipped and understaffed. These examples suggest that social conditions and geography not only affect the higher rates of binge drinking but also affect the lack of treatment for alcohol-related injuries, resulting in higher statistics of alcohol-related problems in Native communities.

Native Treatment

Kelley also notes that since most Native treatment programs are based on the strategies and principles of the dominant culture, participation in treatment programs and treatment success rates are lower than rates for non-Natives. There are numerous reasons for this, but the most significant have to do with cultural differences and acceptance of dominant culture concepts such as "disease model" alcohol education, isolation from family and community and, especially, the emphasis on the Christian-oriented twelve-step program.

Studies have found that alcohol treatment programs for Aboriginal people tend to work better when they focus on traditional Native cultural teachings, traditional settings and traditional self-empowerment programs. Culture and spirituality are the frameworks of treatment developed by First Nations and Inuit communities. The perception of high rates of Native alcoholism is partly grounded in reality, but has mostly been embellished by non-Aboriginals who have not been exposed to an accurate depiction of reserves and urban Native communities. As observed by Gary Roberts of the Canadian Centre on Substance Abuse, non-Natives often form their opinions of Native drinking habits based on the small percentage of Native problem drinkers they see on the street.

In the absence of any concrete evidence that Native people

are genetically different and therefore unable to consume alcohol like "regular people," the next logical conclusion would have to be that Native people drink as a means of escape from their overwhelming social problems. This is an unpopular suggestion since many non-Natives are reluctant to believe that Third World conditions and extreme social ills could exist in a place as rich as North America.

It is much easier for non-Aboriginals to cling to the belief that Native people are somehow genetically or culturally defective but if they just pulled up their bootstraps, got with the program and got over it then they wouldn't need to drink. Naturally, this sentiment is based on the mistaken belief that Native people have, and have always had, the same equal opportunities as the rest of North Americans. Unfortunately though, history, statistics and plain old facts will override this idealistic notion every time.

Finally, the most common way that people perpetuate the stereotype that all Natives are alcoholics is through a phenomenon I like to call *I know a Native*, or IKAN for short. Non-Aboriginals all seem to have this magical Native friend whose behaviour confirms every stereotype they wish to perpetrate. This mystery Native friend never pays taxes, is lazy, is always bucking the system, and from sun up to sun down is perpetually drunk. I don't know who these debauched drunken Natives are that so many non-Natives are hanging around with, but it might be a clue that they should probably start looking into their own drinking habits. You know what they say: *Birds of a feather flock together.*

109

RELIGION & RESIDENTIAL SCHOOLS

"Peace pipe dreams"

WHEN I WAS A YOUNG MAN, ONE OF MY FAVOURITE things to do was to travel from my reserve to one of the many summer powwows that were held throughout my province. For those not familiar with powwows, they are gatherings for different Native nations to come together and feast, drum and dance. Historically, it was a time for different tribes and nations to make peace, form alliances, establish trade negotiations or just simply party. Over time the main purpose of powwows has become a little less diplomatic. We young men went to powwows to "hook up," or as we say in Indian country, "go snagging." But the majority of us were too shy to talk to girls, so we usually just hung in the vehicle that brought us, talking about snagging.

One day, a group of us were hanging out in the van discussing a number of earth-shattering pre-teen topics when we were approached by two non-Native gentlemen in white, starched shirts and equally white, starched smiles. They informed us that the day of reckoning was nigh and that our souls were in danger of burning in a fiery pool of sulphur if we did not reject our pagan rituals and accept the Lord Jesus Christ into our hearts. We were twelve years old.

To make their presentation more visual, they handed us a placemat-sized illustration of what the kingdom of God looked like. Apparently this religion had topographers who went to heaven, mapped it out and returned to earth with a divine blueprint — it was a miracle! In case you've wondered what awaits you in the afterlife, the illustrated diagram revealed heaven as a large amusement park. You heard me: heaven is full of carny rides and from the looks of it, it's not really worth the price of admission. There was one interesting attraction: a Tunnel of Love–type ride that takes you through the miracle of childbirth. Since this religion believes that life begins at conception, I'm assuming the ride begins the moment you stand in the lineup.

Back then our reaction was to roll our eyes (the pre-teen reaction to everything), thank them and send them on their way. We didn't realize it at the time, but we had just been victims of an attempted missionizing, a drive-by saving, a sneak-attack conversion... Sure, they weren't black-robed Jesuits or wild-eyed clerics hauling us off to residential school, but they made it apparent that after five hundred years of interaction with Native people, some Western religions still hadn't changed their tune. We Indians were sinful heathens participating in sinful pagan rituals, and we needed to be saved from our sinful ways. Ironically, if they had just shown us an illustrated picture on how to sin with girls they might have had some easy converts.

Every religion believes that its way is the one true way. Even many Natives believe our way is the one true way. The difference is there aren't a lot of religions that would go into another religion's place of worship, as ceremonies are taking place, and actively try to convert. People have gone missing for less. Unfortunately, Native people still contend with the stereotype that our beliefs and religious practices are a thing of the past and we are holding onto a primitive belief system that prevents us from moving into the twenty-first century. In other words, "Get a real religion, Indians!"

On the flip side there are many people, Native and non-Native, who have romanticized our beliefs so much that any sign of Western or twenty-first century influence would be considered blasphemous. The result has been dogmatic rules surrounding our ceremonial practices that exclude elements that might be deemed "white," i.e. using only matches instead of lighters to ignite sweetgrass, or insisting that water in sweat lodge ceremonies come from a naturally flowing source like a creek or river. Don't get me wrong. I totally respect this adherence to the purity of ceremonies in their pre-contact form, but part of me also thinks, "C'mon, even the Amish ride on airplanes now and again."

The perception that Native religions are simplistic and primitive can be linked to their representation in practically every form of media. Those who romanticize Native religions uphold a version of Native spirituality in which all "real Indians" worship rocks and trees, disappear into thin air when you turn your back, and converse with animals like Doctor Dolittle. In the movies even our youth can't just be regular teenagers; they also have to be shirtless, shape-shifting werewolves. This representation of Native spirituality based in fantasy and mysticism continues to paint our people as superstitious primitives or pagan wizards.

Thanks to our old friend Pan-Indianism, another stereotype insists that all Native people believe the same thing. In addition, textbooks and scholars will often highlight Native myths and legends as though they were the basis of Native religion. This is a strange presumption considering most Native people today understand that our myths and creation stories were allegories and not literal belief systems. You would be hard-pressed to find any Native people embarking on archeological expeditions to search for Glooscap's birthplace, or the village where Frog lost his tail. In contrast, there is an obscene amount of money and research spent on trying to uncover biblical artifacts like Noah's Ark or the Tower of Babel, even when religious scholars have provided volumes of evidence pointing to the allegorical nature of the bible. Nevertheless, it is Native spiritual beliefs that continue to be viewed as primitive, out of touch and simplistic.

113

Native Religion—In a Nutshell

Since there are a lot of misconceptions about what Native religion isn't, let's try to sum up what Native religion *is*. Remember, this is a very broad attempt at explaining common fundamentals of Native spirituality and is not intended to lump all Native spirituality into one Pan-Indian religion. Native religions are as diverse as the people who practise them. Some Native religions are practised by only one nation, and some are practised by a variety of nations. The Native American Church is an example of a religion that is followed by a number of different tribes from a wide array of spiritual traditions. Despite the numerous religious practices across North America, there are some general similarities that fall under the broad-umbrella definition of "Native religion."

At the time of European contact, Native North Americans had very structured religious systems that included cosmology and creation myths that explained the origins of those societies. Native religions are land-based, and their practices and beliefs derive from the environment in which a tribe originates. Many Native religions share the following beliefs and practices: an ever-present universal force, spirits, visions, medicine people, communal ceremony and the "four stages of life": birth, childhood, adulthood and death. Native spiritualities are often characterized by animism. This does not mean we worship animals; it is the belief that natural physical entities including animals, plants and other phenomena possess a spiritual essence. The Japanese religion Shinto is another religion that is highly animistic. The other common thread is panentheism, which is a belief that the divine is in every part of nature and timelessly extends beyond it. In Native panentheism, there is an emphasis on personal spirituality, which is absorbed into the daily life of the believer and focuses on a balance between the natural and spiritual "worlds."

Most would describe Native religions as a "one-ness" or "balance" with creation as opposed to many religions that place God at the top of a symbolic pyramid, followed by man, who holds dominance over the rest of creation. This principle is often found in monotheist or "one god" religions. Monotheism can be found in some of the major religions like Christianity, Islam, Judaism and Sikhism. Even though I use the term "Native religion," those who practise their traditional beliefs view it as more of a journey or process to achieve balance with the Creator and creation, and not a codified religion per se. For Native people, religion does not require a temple or place of worship or a religious text since Native religious practice is not separated from daily life. The very act of living is a form of worship and maintaining a relationship with all of creation is equivalent to a relationship with "God."

Most Native peoples believed in an all-powerful, all-knowing Creator or "Great Spirit" (who existed in every form and gender). They also believed in minor supernatural entities, including evil beings who were responsible for testing mankind with disasters and suffering. Most tribes believed in an immortal human soul and an afterlife that is a paradise filled to abundance with everything that makes life on earth so awesome! Like pizza parlours that serve unlimited cheese sticks. An example of such a paradise is the "Happy Hunting Grounds"—as it is referred to nowadays by NO INDIAN EVER!

Like all other cultures, Native societies called upon spiritual forces to help them survive and maintain order in their natural and social worlds. Each tribe had its own ceremonies and religious observances dedicated to that purpose. Individuals also participated in rituals involving private prayers or sacrifices of physical items (i.e. furs, medicines, food, skin, flesh, etc.). They also enlisted the help of shamans, priests and in some tribes priestesses to access divine assistance in ensuring a bountiful hunt, a successful harvest or victory over enemies.

Many perceive Native religious practices as primitive or fanciful, but what they fail to realize is Native religions bear striking resemblances to early European religions. In her essay "Native American Religion in Early America," Christine Leigh Heyrman observes that these religions also had a creation myth, prayed to a creator, feared a lesser but evil deity and sought to secure a place for the soul in a heavenly amusement park. They also placated their divine being with prayers and offerings, and relied on religious practitioners or clergy to help their societies during periods of crisis.

Native spirituality also does not distinguish between the worlds of the living or dead, visible or invisible, past or present, and heaven or earth. Native spiritual practitioners view all realms as part of one cosmic whole. Most people who practise traditional Indian ways view their whole culture and social structure as infused with "spirituality." Got it? It's important to reiterate that there are many different beliefs and religions practised by Native people including the most widely incorporated religion by Native people today.

Christianity

The Canadian and US governments originally used Christianity as a form of cultural assimilation. Even though the intended goal was to sway Native people into full conversion, instead many Native Christians developed a balance between their traditional beliefs and Christianity. For example, St. David Pendleton Oakerhater was a Cheyenne sun dancer but was also canonized as an episcopal saint.

When it comes to the Christianization of Native people, history has often portrayed two extreme scenarios. The first is that Christianity was forced upon Native populations by unrelenting missionaries. The second was that Native people willingly abandoned their traditions in preference for the dominant Christian faith. In both these scenarios, the assumption is that Christianity rendered Native religion extinct, which further perpetrates the stereotype of the vanishing Indian. Although loss of Native religion and traditions definitely occurred, what is frequently overlooked is the adaptive nature of Native societies and their ability to incorporate Western ideas into their own beliefs.

Many of the parables, characters and creation myths that appear in the bible also appear in other societies that had no previous contact with biblical cultures. For example, the great flood in the book of Genesis also appears in creation stories of practically every culture in the world. Stories of prophets and healers, death and resurrection, and an *End of Days* scenario are common in practically every other world culture that had no previous contact with Judeo-Christian traditions. The names in these First Nations creation stories may be different but the story remains the same. There have been a number of proposed reasons for these similarities in origin stories around the world:

1) Major events occurred that affected the entire globe and every culture recorded the same event using their own cultural

understanding. For example, a great flood, a massive famine or widespread pestilence could have happened on a global level and each society retold the same event using their own cultural archetypes; or

2) The Judeo-Christian bible is the one true religion, and spread its message and parables to every corner of the world in spiritual form long before actual human contact between these cultures existed; or

3) Aliens!

Regardless of whether you believe the scientific, the spiritual or the extraterrestrial version of religious archetypes, an open-minded reading of religious texts will reveal many similarities between the philosophies of the bible and of First Nations religions. However, I said "open-minded," so I wouldn't hold my breath for a favourable comparison between Christianity and First Nations religions anytime soon.

Despite the parallels between religions of Native North Americans and early Europeans, Christine Leigh Heyrman also documents significant differences. The most important is that Natives did not make a distinction between the natural and the supernatural. In fact, Natives viewed the material and spiritual as a unified realm of existence. By contrast, European religions tended to stress the divide between pious spiritual beings in heaven (i.e. God, the angels and saints) — from men and women born into original sin and forced to endure a wicked world filled with temptation, evil and blasphemy (i.e. Toronto). The reason so many perceive Christianity and Native spirituality as polar opposites is not because of widely opposing philosophies, but because of the brutal implementation of Christian doctrines on Native societies. Consequently, the view of many present-day Natives toward Christianity is best echoed in words attributed to Mahatma Gandhi: "I like your Christ. I do not like your Christians. They are so unlike your Christ."

Christianative Religions

Until recently, history tended to view the relationship between Natives and colonists in one of two ways; either as a triumph of "civilization" over Indian "savagery" or a condemnation of genocide of Native peoples through military aggression or disease. In either version, Native people were viewed as passive victims. More recent histories have begun to recognize the ongoing Indian resistance to Euro–North American colonization and especially to forms of cultural adaptation and accommodation that still exists in Native communities today. This is especially true when it comes to the merging of Christian teachings and traditional Native spirituality or, as I like to call them, "Christianative" religions.

These belief systems that have incorporated Christian tenets into Native traditions include the Longhouse religion founded in 1799 by Seneca leader Handsome Lake; the Indian Shaker religion, named for the shaking and twitching motions of the followers to cast off their sins; the Peyote religion, a religious movement that involves the ritual consumption of the peyote cactus; the Feather religion in the Pacific Northwest, so named because eagle feathers are used in the ceremonies; and the Washat/Dreamer Faith that believed that if followers lived a life of non-violence, turned their backs on white culture, and be forbidden to buy, sell or disrespect the Earth that all white people would disappear and the Americas would return to their original state.

The Dreamer Faith foreshadowed the Ghost Dance, which refers to a number of revitalization movements in the western US during the late 1800s. The Ghost Dances were intended to reconnect Native people with their pre-contact traditions, and focused on honouring the dead while also predicting their resurrection. (And no, I don't mean in that overused walking-dead, feast-on-your-brains, zombie kind of way.) The Ghost Dance spread to a

118

number of tribes on reservations throughout the West. During the Indian Wars, the Lakota and Dakota were so desperate for hope that they interpreted the Ghost Dance gospel as a call for the complete elimination of all white people. In December of 1890, a Ghost Dance gathering led to the infamous massacre at Wounded Knee where the Native participants believed their Ghost Dance shirts could stop bullets. The Caddo Nation of Oklahoma still practises the Ghost Dance today.

Despite occurrences of the mixing of Christianity and Native spirituality, at the start of North American history many Natives were reluctant to fully convert. This came as a shock to early missionaries who believed that no civilized person would ever reject the "truth" of Christianity. So, early converters resorted to extreme measures in order to force early Natives to accept the love of Jesus Christ. This became more widespread as the residential and boarding schools were established, and the atrocities that occurred in these schools fell under the purview of official government and church policy.

119

Residential Schools

The Indian residential schools were established before Confederation but became commonplace after the Indian Act was passed in 1876. The schools were funded by the Department of Indian Affairs and were run by Christian churches, especially the Catholic and Anglican Church. By 1931 there were eighty residential schools across Canada and the last residential school didn't close until 1996. The total number of First Nations children that passed through the residential school system is estimated to have been around 150,000.

Over the years there has been much debate about the conditions experienced by the students in residential schools. However, in the early twenty-first century it was officially recognized that residential schools did significant harm to Aboriginal children by snatching them from their families and communities, banning their languages, and forcing them to endure physical and sexual abuse by staff and other students. A primary goal of the schools has been described as "killing the Indian in the child" or more specifically, cultural genocide.

The residential school system was born out of the 1857 Gradual Civilization Act and the 1869 Gradual Enfranchisement Act. Both these acts were created to assimilate Indians into Christianity, training them to become farmers and wiping out Indian languages so they only spoke English. As these laws were being enforced, Native leaders fought like crazy to have them overturned, despite recent attempts at revisionist history that suggest these policies were widely embraced by Native people. Further laws also allowed the residential schools to perform compulsory sterilizations on Native students in a number of provinces. It's interesting to note that around this time Canada went to war in Europe to end Nazi atrocities that included similar forced sterilization on Jews in concentration camps. So, in other words: European sterilization — bad; Indian sterilization — government-funded policy.

Since the schools operated in relative isolation and were largely unmonitored, acts of physical and sexual abuse reached epidemic proportions. Students were severely punished and often beaten for speaking their languages and practising their religions. Corporal punishment was excused as the only viable way to "civilize" the savage or punish runaways. Inadequate living conditions and practically non-existent medical services led to astronomical rates of illness and death by influenza and tuberculosis. Over the course of the century, reports by physicians reported disturbing rates of tuberculosis among students and death rates in some residential schools of up to thirty to sixty percent. To put this in perspective, imagine enrolling your child in grade one and by grade five up to sixty percent of your child's classmates had died — maybe even your own child among them.

Recent published findings have revealed that during the 1940s malnutrition experiments were carried out on approximately one thousand hungry Aboriginal children in six residential schools. These schools cut back milk rations, withheld vitamins and supplements, and even tried out a special enriched flour that couldn't legally be sold anywhere else in Canada. So for those of you who abhor the amount of cruel animal testing they used to do back in the day, you can take some comfort in knowing that sometimes animals were spared in favour of cruel Native child testing.

In 2013, a report by the Truth and Reconciliation Commission found that at least three thousand students had died in the residential schools, mostly from disease. According to the Commission's research and substantiated by a legal report from the Canadian Bar Association, "Student deaths were not uncommon," and a large number of those deaths were not reported back to their families. In some cases, parents were lied to and told their children ran away, never to be seen again. In other cases, children were simply buried onsite in unmarked graves.

Although the residential schools may seem like just another function of the government, the reason they are included in a chapter about religion is because the Christian element and the imposition of those doctrines were the most pervasive of the cruelties that children suffered in the schools. While the federal government may have been funding the schools, they pretty much left it up to the school administrators to determine what would be taught and how. As a result, the schools focused heavily on the complete erasure of Native spirituality and significantly altered the message and practice of Native spirituality to this day.

Through their policies of systematic cultural genocide, the residential schools were largely responsible for the widespread loss of Aboriginal culture and languages. Consequently, the prevalence of post-traumatic stress disorder, drug abuse, alcoholism, violence, domestic abuse and incarceration, have become areas of greater concern in Aboriginal communities than in other cultures within Canada. The children of residential school survivors are also at greater risk for drug and alcohol abuse than children in other cultures due to the "intergenerational legacy" of abuses suffered in the schools.

The effects of Christianity, or what Native people identify with Christianity, has had a profound effect on the way Native people view religion. The physical and sexual violence inflicted on so many Native people has led to a widespread backlash against not only Catholicism and Christianity but also to organized religion in general. This has been a huge problem among Native people who seek help with alcohol and drug addictions because of the God-centred belief system of twelve-step programs.

More significant is the blurring of traditional belief systems with Christian dogma. For example, matrilineal cultures and equality with women were historic principles of Native society and religion, but there have been recent examples of Native ceremonies becoming male-only events. There are many reasons and many ceremonies that are traditionally segregated, but most of these modern separation practices seem to embody a fundamentalist Western approach. Covering one's body as an act of humility has become commonplace in Native ceremonies, which seems counter to traditional cultures where the body was not shamed. The residential school legacy has also led to widespread shame and suppression of Native sexuality, a practice that has little or no basis in traditional Native societies.

The Residential School Legacy

In recent years the federal government, the RCMP, the University of Manitoba and even the Pope—*yes, the Pope!*—have all acknowledged the destructive and genocidal legacy of the residential school systems. In 1998 the government established the Aboriginal Healing Foundation, which provided $350 million to fund community-based healing projects to overcome the school's legacy of physical and sexual abuse. In 2003, the Alternative Dispute Resolution process (ADR) was launched as a process outside of the court system to provide compensation and psychological support for residential school students who were physically or sexually abused or wrongfully confined. And in 2005, the Canadian government announced a compensatory package of $1.9 billion for tens of thousands of former residential school students. At this time, Justice Minister Irwin Cotler called the residential schools "the single most harmful, disgraceful and racist act in our history."

It's puzzling then that so many Canadians still think that residential schools weren't a big deal and Natives should quit whining about it. Did I mention THE POPE acknowledged wrongdoings?! The frickin' POPE! Unfortunately, the "get over it" sentiment continues among non-Natives who are unable to grasp the severity of what occurred during this era of Canadian history. Dismissing residential school trauma as a whiny attempt to access government handouts is yet another example of Native people being regarded as "the other" and unworthy of the same human rights considerations as non-Natives. In fact, these human rights violations continue to be dismissed even in light of recent evidence that Native children were also used as guinea pigs in government-funded starvation experiments.

I guess it's easy for people who have not gone through the

residential school experience to say, "Get over it." Especially when their own experiences with boarding schools only involved an occasional rap on the knuckles by a strict nun with a ruler. However, it's important to reiterate that residential schools were not just boarding schools or private schools. Residential schools were designed specifically to assimilate Indians into European culture. Duncan Campbell Scott, the deputy superintendent of the Department of Indian Affairs from 1913–1932, stated, "I want to get rid of the Indian problem. ... Our objective is to continue until there is not a single Indian in Canada that has not been absorbed into the body politic and there is no Indian Question and no Indian Department."

There are a lot of people who would suggest the policy was "well-meaning" — that the government was trying to help the Natives become productive members of the new and improved Canada. I'd really like to believe that. I'd like to believe that beating the Indian language out of children was just an early precursor to "Hooked on Phonics" or by cutting off the children's hair, which is sacred to Native people, they were just doing a makeover à la *America's Next Top Model*. I'd like to believe that the physical and sexual abuse that occurred in epidemic proportions in these schools was just a simple misunderstanding based on the fact that since the children hadn't denounced their heathen ways and accepted full Christianity, they weren't yet considered humans, so the rampant abuse and rape of these children wasn't technically a sin. I'd like to believe that taking nomadic hunters and gatherers and forcing them to become farmers was to prepare them to be competitive in the Canadian economy. The only problem is, at the time it was illegal for Natives to sell their crops off-reserve because white farmers were afraid of Native competition.

"Hey Grey Bear, wanna buy a potato?"

"Sorry Red Eagle, I got no money. Wanna buy a zucchini?"

"Sorry Grey Bear, I got no money. Boy, this whole farming thing is really working great, eh?"

I'd like to believe that teaching Native children about the parliamentary system was going to help them become active in political issues — except that it was illegal for Indians to vote back then. And I'd like to believe that teaching geography would make those Native children aware of the vast and wondrous world that lay outside the confines of their reservations, except that Natives were literally *confined* to their reserves and had to get permission from an Indian agent to leave. I'd *really* like to believe that assimilation was the primary intent of residential schools, but I have never been one to let blind faith get in the way of the facts. Even a brief skimming of history would suggest that the actual intent of the government was to isolate Native people from Canadian society until they gave up, renounced their treaty status, or more preferably, simply died off. There didn't seem to be any real desire to educate Natives so they could assimilate because assimilation wasn't even an option back then.

Case in point: a few years ago there was a story in the newspaper about a resort in Ontario's cottage country. During the Second World War, the resort was used to house German POWs, but this was no ordinary POW camp. The German captives were allowed to swim freely in the lake and frolic on the beach — a beach that had been illegal for Indians to set foot on. The German POWs were also allowed to go to the movies a couple times a week. They were allowed to sit in the front rows while the Indians were forced to sit in the balconies because Indians couldn't sit with regular folk. Even our enemy captives were allowed greater liberties than Canada's original people. And this was happening during the same war that thousands of Native people were fighting and dying in, only to come home and find their Status rights had been taken away, and their children had been stolen by Social Services and given to foster homes. They weren't even awarded the same promised benefits that non-Native soldiers received when they returned home. Natives were constantly denied the very rights and freedoms that they put their lives on the line for.

This wasn't the American Deep South either, this was Canada. Home of the Underground Railroad. The Promised Land. Former black slaves were afforded liberties that Native people didn't even know existed. And this wasn't a long time ago either, as many people would like to suggest; this was my grandfather's generation and my father's generation — the same generations that went to residential school. When my father was still alive he only told me a few stories about his time at residential school. It was obvious the scars still ran deep. One story he told was about being a small boy herded into the back of a truck with a bunch of other Native children like cattle and driven far away to the Kamloops Indian Residential School. He told me about how one day he escaped from the school and walked over fifty kilometres back home to the reserve. As he walked down the dusty roads of the village, all the adults on the reserve came outside to watch in awe as he walked by. This was the first child any of them had seen in almost a year.

My father was known as a residential school survivor. The reason they're called *survivors* is because many of the children who went to residential schools didn't make it past their first year, both emotionally and physically. A number of children who died while in the schools were buried on-site, sometimes with nothing more than a simple marker to prove they ever existed. Many of them, while still children, committed suicide or died from exposure or heat exhaustion trying to escape. Some of them were beaten so badly at the hands of nuns and priests that if their deaths occurred in any other place it would easily be considered homicide. The majority of these incidents were filed as mere accidents. On a daily basis, the children were humiliated and degraded. They were told that they were nothing but dirty, stupid little Indians. They were told that their parents were ignorant savages, their communities were irrelevant, and their culture, religion and language were the work of the devil. The children were to renounce everything Indian or burn in hell for all eternity.

Now imagine your own children for a moment. Imagine the extent of psychological damage such an experience would have on your son or daughter. Imagine how deeply embedded the self-loathing they would have inside them, the shame and disgust for you as parents because of the cultural and religious ideals you instilled in them. Imagine your children hating you because they were brainwashed into believing you were useless and irrelevant. Imagine your children enduring a lifetime of emotional torture, mistrust and hatred. It's heartbreaking to think of your child that way, isn't it?

Now imagine the people who did this to your children told you it was for their own good and it was making them productive members of society. And imagine people telling you that your children's abuse was in the past and they should just get over it. That's what residential school survivors are told all the time. That's what my father was told, and he dealt with his abuse the same way the vast majority of other residential school survivors did: through drugs, alcohol, violence, self-destruction and eventually jail.

My father was lucky, after years of self-destruction he became involved in Indian activism and began practising his Native spiritual beliefs. Ironically, the same belief system that the residential schools tried to beat out of him was the same belief system that saved his life. Other residential school survivors were not so lucky. Many of them drowned in alcoholism and drug abuse, ending up on the streets or repeating the sexual abuse and violence that was inflicted on them when they were children. And somewhere during all their turmoil and self-destruction, they gave birth to my generation and the generation of Native kids that are in classrooms right now. These Native students learned from their parents that white people are evil, religion is fake, education is designed to destroy our Aboriginality, the law is skewed in favour of those with money, the government is not to be trusted and the Canadian dream is there for everyone but First Nations people. We don't matter, nobody wants us and so what's the point?

As Native kids look around this country, it's pretty easy for them to agree. We have the highest rate of incarceration per capita, the highest rate of suicide, the highest rate of unemployment, the highest rate of high school dropouts, the highest rate of children in foster care (half of all of them), the highest rates of domestic abuse, and we are three times more likely than non-Natives to commit homicide... I guess if I tried to put a positive spin on these statistics I could say, "We're number one, we're number one..." With half the Native population today under the age of twenty-five and violent crime and gangs increasing in our communities, it's a pretty scary time to be an Aboriginal youth in this country. This is the baggage that Native children live with each and every day.

Now I ask, if the residential school legacy had been inflicted on non-Native children instead of Aboriginal children, how many people would still insist that they should just "get over it"? I'm guessing not too many. I've witnessed way too many non-Native people lose their minds in Starbucks and scream bloody murder just for not getting enough foam on their latte.

Native Religion Outlawed

Not only was Native religion suppressed in residential schools, it was also banned throughout the rest of North America. Freedom of religion has been one of the founding precepts since the inception of the United States and Canada; however, this basic constitutional right has been repeatedly denied to Native people. In fact, the whole concept of separating church and state was completely ignored when it came to dealings with Indian people and quite often Christianity was used as a tool in implementing government policy. Back in those days, it should have been clarified that "religious freedom" really meant, "If your religion is Christian, then Indian land is free."

For American Indian Heritage Month in the US, writer James Thull documented the history of laws attempting to ban Native religions, starting with Secretary of the Interior Henry M. Teller. In 1882 Teller tried to put an end to all "heathenish dances and ceremonies," referring to them as a "great hindrance to civilization." For a bit of perspective, this is also what US politicians said when Chubby Checker first introduced the twist. The following year, in 1883, US Commissioner of Indian Affairs Hiram Price officially banned Native religion by introducing the Indian Religious Crimes Code. Ten years later, the new Commissioner of Indian Affairs Thomas J. Morgan continued the persecution of Native religions by charging people up to six months in jail if they continued to act as a medicine man or participated in religious dances. Wow, six months in jail for dancing? And those kids in *Footloose* thought *they* had it bad. Not long after, Canada followed suit and also banned the majority of First Nations religious practices.

Thull recalled that the government's attempts to suppress Native religions led to one of the bloodiest events in US history: the Massacre at Wounded Knee. On December 29, 1890, the Seventh Calvary rode into the Lakota Sioux's Pine Ridge and Rosebud reservations to enforce the ban on a Ghost Dance and arrest the participants. That was the official story at the time, but it just so happened that the Seventh Calvary was the former unit of General Custer who was recently killed at the Battle of Little

129

Bighorn. It is now believed that the Seventh Cavalry used the ban on Native religious dances as an excuse to exact revenge on the Sioux who were partly responsible for the death of their general. Regardless, a dispute over a firearm ensued and the cavalry attacked and murdered approximately 150 Native American men, women and children. Every member of the Seventh Cavalry was brought up on charges of killing innocents, but every single one of them was exonerated. The massacre essentially put an end to the widespread Ghost Dance movement and is considered by many historians to mark the end of the Indian Wars.

American Indian Religious Freedom Act (AIRFA)

In 1978, the US Congress passed AIRFA, which was designed to remove government control over Native American religions. The act dealt with contentious issues like granting access to sacred Native sites, peyote use, the freedom of Native American prisoners to practise their religions, and the repatriation of ceremonial artifacts and human remains. Until AIRFA, Native Americans could technically be jailed for up to thirty years just for practising their rituals. In fact, the sacred Sun Dance was illegal from the 1880s (Canada) and 1904 (USA) up until the 1980s. In the US, the legality of possessing eagle feathers, using ceremonial peyote, and the repatriation of human remains and cultural artifacts continue to be challenged in the courts.

The eagle feather law, which deals with the religious possession and use of eagle feathers, was enacted to protect the once-dwindling eagle populations. At the same time, it attempted to protect the widespread use of eagle feathers in Native American religious customs. As a result, the possession of eagle feathers is restricted solely for the use of Native Americans. This policy has enraged people on all sides of the debate but mostly from those who love to sing their favourite song, "Natives Always Get Special Treatment!" (For a lot of people, that's a very catchy tune.) The Native American Graves Protection and Repatriation Act, or NAGPRA (not the cleverest acronym), was passed in 1990 and gave Native people a way to request the return or "repatriation" of human remains and cultural and religious items. Even though there have been significant legal and constitutional efforts to protect Native religion and promote understanding, there are still numerous misconceptions about Native ceremonial practices.

Ceremonial Pipes

Movies and television have been responsible for many of the stereotypes about Native pipes, starting with the name "peace pipe." In actuality, they are called "ceremonial pipes" because they are often used in — you guessed it — ceremonies. The pipe is often smoked in these gatherings because it is believed that the smoke carries the participant's words and prayers up to the Creator. Not everyone can possess a pipe for ceremony. There is a lifetime of spiritual training that goes into being able to possess a pipe. Once a person is deemed worthy, that person becomes a pipe carrier and is held in a very sacred trust amongst Native people. In Native spirituality, to be a pipe carrier is a very sacred tradition, which is why the following stereotype is so annoying...

Whether it's just uninformed assumptions or wishful thinking, there is a belief that ceremonial pipes are filled to the brim with hallucinogens. This stereotype is illustrated in movies like *Shanghai Noon* where Jackie Chan and Owen Wilson take part in a pipe ceremony and end up giggly stoned. While this may seem like harmless comedy, it is indicative of a commonly held belief that most Native ceremonies revolve around drug use. Nothing could be further from the truth. The reality is that Jackie Chan and Owen Wilson would not have gotten high because ceremonial pipes are loaded strictly with tobacco. Yep, that's it—just tobacco! As a matter of fact, back in the *Shanghai Noon* days they probably wouldn't even have gotten a head rush, as the tobacco used by Indians was a mixture of naturally occurring leaves and was not laced with the hundreds of unnatural chemicals that are found in modern-day tobacco.

The stereotype of dope-smoking Indians having visions because they are all "Snoop Doggy" has been used to frighten people into believing that Native spiritual practices are dangerous, hallucinogenic, pagan religions à la *Reefer Madness*. On the contrary, with the exception of the peyote-based religions that are controlled in their ceremonial execution, most Native communities ban the use of alcohol and drugs during their ceremonies. While most Native belief systems do not believe that alcohol or drugs are bad in their natural form, most believe that it is important to approach prayer and ceremonies with an unclouded heart and mind so that your thoughts and intentions will be clean and honest. So for those of you that want to stop at an Indian ceremony on your way to a Phish concert, give your eyes a few drops of Visine and leave your Zig Zags in the car. (And get a haircut, damn hippies.)

Peyote

Possible reasons for the misconception that Native religions are drug-based stems from the misconceptions about peyote. When people discover that I am Native, I am frequently asked, "What is peyote like?"—as if every newborn Native child was issued a birth certificate and a button of peyote at the hospital. (I have *not* tried peyote by the way.) In case you're not hip to the jive (or whatever the kids are saying these days), peyote is a small, spineless cactus from the southwestern US and Mexico that possesses the psychedelic mescaline. The "buttons" can be chewed, or boiled in water and drunk as a tea. Peyote often gets a bad rap but what many people don't know is that for centuries it was used by some Native tribes for its medicinal properties.

Peyote use is legal and "racially" neutral in the United States as long as it is taken by members of the Native American Church. This means non-Natives can also use peyote as long as it is used within the parameters of a Native American ceremony. However, any manufacturers or suppliers of peyote for the Native American Church are required to obtain a licence and comply with the requirements of the law. A peyote licence, huh? I bet you don't want to accidentally hand that one to a cop at a random traffic stop.

In Canada, possession of peyote is legal just as long as you don't intend to consume the plants or seeds. Otherwise your lawyer might insist you plead to the popular "just holdin' it for a friend" defense. Canada also allows peyote to be used in a religious context as long as it is for a recognized peyote religion. So, taking peyote before heading out to your synagogue is not only illegal, it would break your poor mother's heart. Oy, and you used to be such a good little boychick, too, before you started dating that shiksa!

So even though the use of peyote is allowed for certain medicinal and ceremonial purposes, according to the law and most peyote spiritualists, going out to the desert with a bunch of buddies and tripping out on peyote does not make the act legal. It also does not constitute an authentic Native ceremony. I hate to burst your bubble, but you're not engaging in Native spirituality and you can't actually see the music. You're just high, dude. Drink lots of water and don't operate heavy machinery for at least eight hours. (And get a haircut, damn hippies.)

Internet Shamans

Natives are usually willing to talk about their spiritual beliefs under the right circumstances. Unfortunately, so are plenty of uninformed, self-proclaimed, non-Native (or people of Native descent) "shamans" who are pushing a version of Native spirituality that has no basis in actual traditional practices. In addition, there are plenty of unscrupulous souls trying to make a buck or get a little attention. A red flag of an inauthentic Native spiritualist includes the offer to sell anything spiritual. Authentic spiritual leaders almost never charge money for religious Native ceremonies like sweat lodges or sun dances or for religious items like a medicine pouch. A promise to guide you through a vision quest through your web browser is also laughable. Another red flag is making you an honorary tribal member or inviting you into their religion through the internet.

Many authentic Native spiritualists will use the internet to educate strangers but the actual act of adopting someone into the culture or inviting them into Native spiritual practices can only be done in person and could take years of getting to know the person. The only way to "join" a Native spiritual tradition is to integrate with that cultural group and you can't do that via WiFi. In case you have ever considered receiving Native spiritual instruction over the internet for a fee, just heed this little bit of Native wisdom: *There are no Indian words for "PayPal."*

Naturally, there are exceptions to these "rules," and I might be a little hypersensitive about Native hucksters since my father was a pipe carrier, but it can also be extremely dangerous, both spiritually and physically, to engage in Native religious practices without the guidance of a trained spiritual leader. This was especially true in the case of New Age guru James Arthur Ray, who built a multimillion-dollar business as a bestselling author and motivational coach. In 2009 Ray, who has no training or affiliation in any Native spiritual traditions, lured his followers into the deserts of Arizona where they meditated in the sun for thirty-six hours without food and water. He then conducted a sweat lodge ceremony with his fifty-five followers where three people died from overheating and nineteen others were hospitalized. Ray was found negligent, but acquitted of manslaughter charges that could have sent him to prison for thirty years. Ironically, that is the same amount of time that real Native spiritualists could have spent in prison just for practising their traditions properly. The moral of the story: Native spiritual practices are done by trained professionals. Don't try this at home!

135

Women and Ceremonies

Women in traditional Native societies were revered for their ability to give life. An aspect of this was the woman's menstrual cycle, which was honoured for its spiritual power. As a result there were certain traditions that separated women from the community during this sacred time of the month. Modern-day female rights activists will leap on these exemptions as sexist or anti-feminist because they mistakenly liken the Native view of menstruation with that of the European traditions, where menstruation was considered unclean and impure; Native traditions surrounding this issue are the exact opposite.

A woman's menstrual cycle is often compared to the moon's lunar cycle in that its cycle culminates in a full moon just as a woman's monthly cycle culminates in menstruation. That is why you'll often hear of a woman's menstrual flow being referred to as her "moon time." It is believed that her restorative process is so strong during this time that it is able to draw power away from the ceremonies, sacred items and foods that are eaten during and after ceremonies. During this time, Native women would retire to a moon lodge in order to rest and receive guidance from the Creator. Many likened this time to a sort of vision quest and the people of the village would respect and honour these women by taking over their workload or cooking for them and protecting them. This nurturing approach to menstruation is the opposite of patriarchal societies in which women's bleeding is considered a curse and something to be ashamed of.

To sum up, the stereotype of Native people praying to trees, rocks, mountains or other inanimate objects is a fallacy based on Eurocentric understandings of hierarchal religion. Instead, Native religion focused on the notion of the Creator as present in all of creation, and did not separate creation into that with a soul and that without. The belief that all of creation is an extension of "God" is becoming a widely embraced belief system in Native communities and throughout the world. It appears to be a more sustainable world view when you consider the extent that popular religions have been hijacked in order to justify the mass destruction of the environment, unending wars and countless human rights violations. If attempting to live in balance and harmony with nature and all races of mankind is still considered superstitious and primitive then hand me an eagle feather and call me a savage! I'll gladly embrace that stereotype. And yes, I know what you're thinking: "Get a haircut. Damn hippie."

TREATIES

"Sign on the dotted lie"

THOSE WHO OBSESS ABOUT CANADA'S IDENTITY (OR lack thereof) frequently claim that this country is a perfect mix of American and European culture. I agree. We have American-style cities (i.e. Toronto) minus the crime, dirtiness or—for lack of a better word—excitement that you find in US cities. We have French-style cities (i.e. Montreal) with European sophistication and ridiculously beautiful people, but without the Stone-Age US morality that often targets Quebec's style of avarice. And we have British-style cities (i.e. Victoria) that are famous for... um... naps? Early-bird buffets? I don't know. The point is, Canada has managed to strike a healthy balance between the three cultures that fought to be its baby daddy during its conception. Wait a second, did I say *three* cultures? Actually, there were four main powers that were responsible for the back and forth control of the Great White North and — surprise, surprise — one of those cultures wasn't white. I am referring to the fourth equal power known as Native Nations, who are responsible for the numerous treaties that cover most of Canada's land mass today.

Treaties are an important part of Canadian history: the Treaty of Paris, the Jay Treaty, the Canadian–American Reciprocity Treaty, the North American Free Trade Agreement; these treaties and more continue to shape Canadian life today. Whether people agree with the content of these treaties or not, most would accept that they are legal and constitutionally binding agreements. The reason they are binding is because they were signed between sovereign nations with their own cultures, languages and land base, and the treaties accommodated those differences so nations could co-exist in harmony. As a result, these international treaties are upheld in domestic and international law. What most people don't realize is that Canada also signed treaties with sovereign nations within the borders of their own sovereign nation of Canada. I know right? In the words of Keanu Reeves: "Whoa..."

These sovereign nations with whom Canada signed legal and constitutionally binding treaties were Aboriginal people. Unfortunately, these treaties are often dismissed by those who fail to recognize Aboriginal sovereignty as similar to that of Europe or America. Now I know what you're thinking: "Come on! Are you comparing that broken-down, poverty-stricken reserve near my town to a sovereign nation like America?" Hmmmm... Broken-down? Poverty-stricken? Have you visited America recently?

Despite the seeming lack of sovereignty in Native communities today, it's important to note that Native sovereignty has never been surrendered. Natives are still legally and constitutionally recognized as separate and distinct entities from the rest of Canada. Obviously many people will swear up and down that this should not be the case. Some will even bypass reality altogether and insist that it is not the case. But the proof lies in centuries' worth of treaties that were created the moment Europeans stepped on the shores of Canada and said, "I love the property, I'll take it." Many Canadians assume treaties no longer apply today or are just vague documents that enabled Europeans to snatch up Native land. There are even those who believe the government fulfilled its treaty obligations long ago and Natives are now looking for free benefits they are no longer entitled to. Many Canadians have been sadly misinformed.

Special interest groups have been very effective in stirring up fear and hatred by suggesting treaties give Native people an unfair advantage based on race. They insist that treaties should be done away with, and all Canadians should live under the same rules and laws. This "one law for all" argument is misleading considering it has never applied to actual Canadian law and justice. Since 1774, Quebec has practised French civil law while the rest of Canada practises English common law, but for some reason these "equality" proponents tend to let Quebec slide. In addition, the constitution and the law allows Quebec to give precedence and prominence of the French language over English in a very unequal manner. Yet again, when it comes to Quebec these equality folks usually just shrug and say, *vive la différence!* Could this be because Quebec is one of the most politically powerful provinces in Canada?

139

For the record, land and treaty claims are not clogging up the courts just because a bunch of Indians are standing around screaming, "White man stole the land!" Au contraire. In order for land and treaty claims to get to court you also need a bunch of lawyers standing around screaming, "White man stole the land"! (My father-in-law, the lawyer, is going to love that one.) I'm not saying every land and treaty claim is valid. There are some Aboriginals who believe that if they hold a door open for a non-Native, they should be compensated. However, real land claims, real treaty rights and real compensations have all gone through proper legal and constitutional process. The goodwill or kindness of non-Native Canadians has absolutely nothing to do with it.

Think about it logically: any political leader would be lynched if he or she said, "Folks, Native people have no binding agreements that prove we owe them anything. They have no recognized status as sovereign nations. They have no valid claims on land title or special rights in Canada. But hey, let's give them a bunch of free stuff other Canadians don't get! Let's give them land, self-government, and special hunting and fishing rights that will lead to violent clashes between Natives and non-Natives. Not because we are obligated to do so, let's do it because we feel bad. Who's with me?"

Could you imagine the backlash, the rage and the fiery protests? Actually, we're Canadians so it would probably just be a bunch of eye-rolling and passive-aggressive sighs. Regardless, this white guilt notion has led to a prevalent stereotype that treaties give Native people unfair rights in the areas of education funding, housing funding, tax exemption, medical benefits, dental benefits... the list goes on and on. Many non-Natives complain their tax dollars are paying for treaty rights that provide Natives with a life on easy street and endless free stuff. Case in point: when I was a kid, I was bused an hour every morning from my reserve to the local town to attend junior high. One day I was walking down the hallway with a non-Native classmate and he turned to me and said, "You Natives are lucky." Now growing up on a poor and isolated reserve, I was not accustomed to being regarded with envy, so naturally I was confused. "Why am I lucky?" I asked.

"You're lucky," he said, "because all you Natives get free trucks." Huh. Interesting. All the people on my reserve foolishly paid money for their trucks. Was this another bit of information that the federal government was hiding from us? More importantly,

Peace and Friendship Treaties. These treaties did not contain any land surrenders; they were just simple promises that if the French and their allies stepped out of line then the Mi'kmaq and the Maliseet would have Britain's back.

As so often happened in Canada's history, once Britain no longer required protection from the Mi'kmaq, Maliseet and any other "M"-named Natives, they broke the Peace and Friendship Treaties almost immediately. I think it's fair to say that if Britain were a person it would easily be diagnosed with narcissistic personality disorder. Regardless of Britain's serial agreement-breaking, court cases based on the Peace and Friendship Treaties are still **145** being ruled on today. In 1985, the Supreme Court of Canada upheld the validity of the treaties by reversing a conviction against James Simon of the Shubenacadie reserve for hunting out of season. Since hunting and fishing laws fall under the jurisdiction of the provincial government, the ruling reaffirmed the nation-to-nation relationship that Aboriginals share with the federal government. As Eskasoni-based treaty scholar Rena Gayde succinctly put it, "The British, the French, none of them would have entered into a treaty-making enterprise with the Mi'kmaw and Maliseets if they didn't consider us sovereign people."

Seven Years' War

The period between the start of the Seven Years' War in 1756 and the close of the War of 1812 saw North America racked with intense warfare between France and Britain, then between American revolutionaries and Loyalists, and finally between the armies of the United States and British Canada. In all of these conflicts, Aboriginal nations were extremely valuable allies due to their ability to wage war in conditions that were extremely difficult for European soldiers (I guess they were afraid they might get their powdered wigs dirty). North American Indians were largely responsible for altering global power dynamics, and by securing treaties and war alliances they advanced their own interests through foreign policies that still affect the geopolitics of North America to this day. Not bad for a bunch of people who lived in Popsicle-stick teepees.

Still concerned about French–Aboriginal military alliances, in 1755 the British created the Indian Department to strengthen relationships with the Iroquois Confederacy. The Indian Department, led by British Superintendent of Indian Affairs Sir William Johnson and his Iroquois wife Molly Brant, neutralized the French–Aboriginal alliance through a series of treaties that guaranteed British protection of Native lands from American colonists.

The end of the Seven Years' War in 1763 forever changed the relationship between Aboriginals and the British. When the French lost Quebec and Montreal, their Algonquian allies pulled a Switzerland and declared their neutrality in exchange for the continued use of their traditional territories, protection of their villages, protection from the Huron and a trade relationship with Britain. Basically the Algonquian said to the British, "Our alliance with France? Nah, we were just kidding about that. Britain rocks! Soooo... we cool now?" This loss of their Aboriginal allies was a devastating blow to France.

The Royal Proclamation

Pay close attention to this section about the Royal Proclamation because it's a doozy and continues to haunt Canadian governments to this day... After the Seven Years' War, Britain was now the big cheese and held the majority of European power in North America. But its success could only depend on maintaining positive relationships with First Nations. So in 1763, the British created the Royal

Proclamation, which established a boundary to which all lands to the west became "Indian Territories" off-limits to European settlers. Most importantly, the Royal Proclamation established that the Crown and only the Crown could buy land from First Nations people. Any purchase of Indian land had to be done in a public forum through official representatives, so no under-the-table deals could be made. The Royal Proclamation was the first official public recognition of First Nations rights and pre-existing rights to the land. It also set out that the Crown had a fiduciary responsibility to the First Nations whose territory was affected.

The term "fiduciary responsibility" comes up a lot in discussing First Nations/federal government relations. Under British common law, a fiduciary is someone who acts on behalf of another in a relationship of strict trust and confidence. Fiduciaries are expected to be extremely loyal to the people or entities they represent and cannot profit from their positions, or place their personal interests before the principals' interests without their consent. This means that under the Royal Proclamation and British common law, the Crown (Canada) cannot buy, sell or encroach on Indian land without permission from the Indians who own that land. This fiduciary responsibility has been called into question for centuries as the Crown has constantly placed its own interests before the Aboriginals under its fiduciary care and profited from that broken trust. In breaking the terms of its treaty obligations, the Crown is also in violation of its own English laws.

I'm going to remind you of this part again because it's going to be on the test: the Royal Proclamation stated that no individual or colony may buy Indian land directly from the Aboriginal people. Only the Crown could buy land from a First Nation that had agreed to the sale at a public meeting. Got that? Good, because this legal concept will make several appearances throughout the history of Canada. As a result of the Royal Proclamation,

First Nations, Inuit and Metis peoples view treaty agreements as existing between the reigning sovereign of England and not the ever-changing cabinet of Canada. This constitutional relationship recognizing and affirming "existing Aboriginal and treaty rights" was written into section 35 of the Constitution Act of 1982, which is also known as "the supreme law of Canada."

Pre-Confederation Treaties

After the Royal Proclamation and before Confederation in 1867, several treaties were signed including the Upper Canada Treaties (1764 to 1862) and the Vancouver Island Treaties (1850 to 1854). Under these treaties, the First Nations in Ontario and British Columbia exchanged land in return for promised benefits such as reserves, annual or other types of payments, plus — and sing along because you all know the words — certain rights to hunt and fish! Despite instances of land cessation, the Crown was still fairly reliant on First Nations for commercial and military needs. As the British settled throughout the Great Lakes, the primary goal of the Indian Department was to maintain peace between the outnumbered British soldiers and traders and the numerous and armed First Nations.

In 1783 the American War of Independence and creation of the United States had severe impacts on alliances between the British and First Nations. Following the loss of the American colonies, about thirty thousand British Loyalist refugees arrived in Canada demanding land from British administrators. In addition to the onslaught of settlers, many First Nations people who had sided with the British were also forced to leave the new American colonies. Despite the important role of Indians in the war efforts, British diplomats attempted to make room for the new settlers by ignoring the Crown treaties.

In 1783, the Treaty of Paris established a new international border along the Great Lakes that cut through Indian land that had already been protected by treaties. Aboriginal groups refused to accept American control of their lands south of the new border. In 1790 and 1791, a small army of US soldiers were twice defeated by the well-armed Aboriginal forces who essentially made the US their bee-atch! Those major American defeats are sometimes referred to as "Harmar's Humiliation" or "St. Clair's Shame," named after the defeated American generals. In 1793 the US government bowed to the Aboriginal confederacy and British government and relinquished control of lands west of the Ohio River back to the Aboriginal nations. Yeah. Put that in your peace pipe and smoke it.

149

The War of 1812 was one of the most important events in North American history—not only because it inspired the theme song for *The Bad News Bears*, but it was also one of the last major wars between Canada and France on North American soil. Deciding factors in this conflict were the mobilization of soldiers in the Great Lakes and especially the Aboriginal role in the capture of Detroit. I know it's hard to believe, but there was actually a time in this continent's history when people flocked *toward* Detroit. The Aboriginal-led seizure of pre-Motor City enabled the British to move soldiers from the European theatre to Upper Canada and thereby gain the upper hand. These events were a testament to the success of the treaty system of Crown–Aboriginal alliances and were instrumental in the early defence of Canada during the War of 1812. Having said that, you would think the British would be eternally grateful to their Native allies and would honour the treaties they entered into in exchange for the essential Native assistance in furthering British supremacy, right? Right?

Not so fast. As military threats passed with the end of the

War of 1812, so did England's reliance on their First Nation allies. The British now shifted their focus on "civilizing" the indigenous people and forcing them to abandon their traditional ways of life in favour of a more agricultural and British lifestyle. These policies blatantly ignored the treaty promises that Native people could continue to practise their traditional ways of life, including *the right to hunt and fish*. In other words, the British turned out to be — dare I say — a bunch of "Indian givers."

As lands were filled with non-Native settlers, fur trader and elected representative William Robinson had the bright idea to open up the north, especially where minerals had been discovered along Lake Superior and Lake Huron. In 1850, he negotiated two treaties with Aboriginals of the northern Great Lakes. These treaties promised the creation of reserves, annual payments and the continued right to hunt and fish on unoccupied lands. In the same year, Hudson's Bay Company Chief Factor James Douglas, who later became governor of Vancouver Island, negotiated the first of fourteen treaties with the Island's First Nations. These treaties exchanged land around HBC posts for cash payments, goods and — yep — the continued right to hunt and fish. Treaty-making was later restricted in the 1860s when British Columbia refused to recognize Aboriginal land title.

The Indian Act

With the creation of the Dominion of Canada in 1867 came another upheaval in the relationship between the Crown and Aboriginal peoples. The newly created British North America Act included section 91(24), which established that "Indians, and the Lands reserved for the Indians" would now fall under the control of the federal government. This was a major change from the original relationship that Aboriginal people had with the sovereign

Crown. The new Dominion of Canada utilized the Department of Indian Affairs to create national policies that would negatively affect all Aboriginal peoples. These policies were then officially incorporated into the Indian Act between 1868 and 1876.

The updated Indian Act of 1876 gave huge authority to the Department of Indian Affairs such as deciding who could be considered an Indian; controlling Indian lands, resources and finances; controlling access to alcohol; and enforcing British "civilization." Unlike the original fiduciary responsibility of the Crown under the Royal Proclamation, the Indian Act attempted to control Aboriginal people until they completely assimilated into Canadian society. The British no longer needed the First Nations to fight their battles anymore so they were now considered "Bad Indians." As the Indian Act continued to be amended in the subsequent decades, it eventually came to prohibit nearly every aspect of daily life for Aboriginal peoples, altering the co-existence relationship promised in the treaties and relegating Native people to wards of the state.

151

The Numbered Treaties

The first Prime Minister of Canada, Sir John A. Macdonald, (a.k.a. the Dude on the Ten), wanted to create a nation connected by the Canadian Pacific Railway. Before this could happen the government needed to own and settle the southern portions of Rupert's Land surrounding Hudson Bay. In 1869, the Hudson's Bay Company sold the Rupert's Land Charter to Canada, which enabled the country to gain full control of the resources and create the Northwest Territories. The only problem was that Canadian law recognized that those pesky First Nations still held title to those lands.

This was a big deal for the Crown because it needed to gain

control over all of Canada in case the Americans wanted to come in and snatch it up. The Canadian government was also unable to wage war on the Indians, not because it didn't want to but because it was too costly. During the 1800s the US government was spending over $20 million a year fighting the Plains Indians, which was more than the entire budget of the Canadian government. So federal officials relied on treaties to bring about the co-operation of the thirty-five thousand Aboriginal inhabitants in the territories scheduled for settlement.

By the 1870s, the First Nations of the prairies were living in dire conditions. Non-Native hunting in both the Canadian and American West had rendered the Plains bison population all but extinct. First Nations people were also plagued by disease and desperate for food aid and other assistance from the government. It was also made clear that non-Natives would soon be taking control of their lands whether treaty deals were reached or not. The Natives could either fight the newcomers or exchange their land in exchange for government assistance.

Between 1871 and 1921, Aboriginal groups in the prairies signed eleven treaties with the Crown, known as the Numbered Treaties. These were divided into two groups: those for settlement in the south; and those for access to natural resources in the north. In Treaties 1 through 7 the Natives typically sought commitments from the government to build schools on newly created reserves, farm equipment, seeds, farm animals and the prohibition of the liquor trade in Native communities. They also made provisions for hunting and fishing rights (do I even have to say it anymore?), annual payments, initial lump-sum payments and—for some strange reason—medals, flags and chiefs' uniforms.

The most comprehensive of these agreements was Treaty No. 6, including the insistence by Cree negotiators that their people be supplied with a "medicine chest." The "medicine chest clause" has been interpreted to mean that the federal government must provide all forms of healthcare to First Nations on an ongoing basis. Those covered by Treaty No. 6 were also promised that if they were to experience "any pestilence" or "general famine," the Crown would do all that was necessary to relieve them of their hardships. Last I looked, Treaty No. 6 Indians are still waiting for their promised help.

Through the Numbered Treaties, the Crown gained possession of almost half of Canada, secured its position north of the border, opened up the West to settlers and linked British Columbia to the rest of the country. However, not all Aboriginal groups were lovin' the treaty relationships. Even those who supported the treaties disagreed on the type of demands that should be made. Not surprisingly, the Aboriginal leaders who readily embraced the treaties were Christians who frequently allowed their missionaries to act as go-betweens between the First Nations and Crown. Since the missionaries and the Canadian governments were often on the same page as to how the First Nations could best be served (complete assimilation) it's easy to see how the Natives got the short end of the stick. The Metis were also prominent in the treaty process by acting as intermediaries between Aboriginals and the newcomers.

Modern Treaties and Patriation

Meanwhile back at the ranch (BC, the Yukon, Northwest Territories, Quebec and the Maritimes), settlers decided to illegally settle on vast swaths of Indian land without first purchasing Aboriginal title through the Crown. Instead of punishing the settlers for this breach of treaty law, the government just moved Natives onto reserves instead. These reserves became home for Aboriginals who were not part of a negotiated treaty and fell under the administrative control of the Indian Act. Since then, the Indian Act has blurred the distinctions between treaty Indians and registered Indians not covered by treaties, leading to many Canadians being unaware that across large parts of the country, Aboriginal title has never been legally ceded.

Although some treaties were negotiated in the 1850s on Vancouver Island, for the most part officials in BC have refused to accept that Native people on unceded land have inherent Aboriginal rights. The Nisga'a people have long opposed this position. As a result of their activism, the Supreme Court of Canada passed down a split decision in 1973 that Aboriginal title is an identifiable legal interest throughout most of BC. The Supreme Court's ruling on the Nisga'a case forced Aboriginal rights into the public consciousness during the 1970s. Another influential incident was the 1969 introduction of a federal "White Paper" on Aboriginal policy, in which Prime Minister Trudeau pushed to remove special status for Aboriginal people by attempting to close out all treaties. Trudeau's political career was built on opposing special constitutional status for Quebec, and he mistakenly thought Aboriginal rights could be lumped in with those of Quebec. Oh Pierre, you so crazy. The White Paper was strongly opposed by Native people, who became extremely organized and vocal.

The result of Native opposition was a change in federal policy and the creation of an Office of Native Claims to resolve land disputes. The ONC now defines two types of claims: "comprehensive" and "specific." Comprehensive claims deal with those parts of Canada where Aboriginal title has not been dealt with by treaty or any other legal means. They are called "comprehensive" because of their wide scope in dealing with such things as land title, fishing and hunting rights, and financial compensation. Specific Claims deal with issues that have arisen due to Canada's mishandling of historic treaties, or the mismanagement of First Nation funds or assets. For example, the failure to provide enough reserve land as promised in a historic treaty or mishandling of First Nations money by the Crown might be dealt with by a specific claim. The government usually prefers to handle these claims by negotiating individual settlements with First Nations. (You know, hush hush, no cans of worms, keeping it on the down low and the QT — that sort of thing.)

The 1975 James Bay and Northern Quebec Agreement was a modern-day treaty to develop a hydroelectric project on the eastern half of James Bay. The enormous project was initiated in the early 1970s without the permission of the area's Cree and Inuit. Through a hard-fought battle in the courts and the media, the Aboriginal residents of James Bay proved that the project was being pushed through on unceded Aboriginal land. The government came back with its tail between its legs and negotiated an agreement that established a basis for the Cree and Inuit to establish institutions of self-government such as school boards and health and social service agencies, to name a few.

155

In 1980 the Trudeau government was re-elected for a third time, like the endless sequels in the *Friday the Thirteenth* movie franchise. Concerned with the separatist movement in Quebec, Trudeau launched a number of discussions with provincial premiers about repatriating the Canadian constitution. First Nations, Inuit and Metis political organizations tried to get a seat at these constitutional negotiations but were routinely denied. On November 5, 1981, nine provincial governments (excluding Quebec) agreed to enter into Trudeau's patriation plan on one condition — that Aboriginal and treaty rights be stripped from the document. "Damn! Oh no you di'int!"

First Nations, Inuit and Metis organizations circled the wagons (ironically) and after several months of hard lobbying and pressure, managed to have two clauses (section 35) entrenched in the Charter of Rights and Freedoms: a definition of Aboriginal people that included all three groups, and recognition of "existing Aboriginal and treaty rights." Premier Lougheed of Alberta fought hard to include the word "existing" in hopes that it would eventually phase out the legal interpretation of section 35. Alberta did that, eh? Yep, sounds about right.

An important aspect of the Aboriginal position was that Aboriginal and treaty rights were guaranteed by the imperial Crown, and Canada lacked authority to sever the relationship between Native people and the Crown without their consent. The First Nations challenge of the patriation process led to the judgment by British judge Lord Denning in 1982 that treaty relationships were in fact solely between Native people and the Crown in respect of the UK. He also proclaimed that, "No parliament should do anything to lessen the worth of these guarantees." (This is why I have always promised to name my firstborn child Lord Denning. Boy or girl.)

In 1983 a First Ministers Conference was held to give greater definition to section 35 but this time representatives of four national Aboriginal organizations were invited to act as consultants. The result was an accord that constitutionally entrenched "treaty rights" as those that previously existed or would be acquired through land claims agreements. Furthermore, Aboriginal and treaty rights would be "guaranteed equally" to male and female Aboriginals. This stipulation did away with many of the sexist policies that were forced upon Native societies through the Indian Act.

During Brian Mulroney's first term as prime minister he allowed Native land claims to stagnate, which backfired on him during his second term. In 1990 Elijah Harper, an MLA from Manitoba and member of the Red Sucker Lake First Nation, used a procedural manoeuvre to block the Meech Lake Accord, a revision to the Canadian constitution that had been negotiated by eleven first ministers without Aboriginal representation. The next month an argument between the Mohawk of Kanesatake, Quebec, and the town of Oka over a proposed golf course erupted into an armed standoff with massive repercussions for Aboriginal and non-Aboriginal relations across Canada.

In order to mend relations, a Royal Commission on Aboriginal Peoples was formed in 1991 just as a surge of modern-day treaty-making took force. This surge was particularly evident in 1993 and 1994 in the north, where negotiations led to the Gwich'in Comprehensive Land Claim Agreement, the Sahtu Dene and Metis Comprehensive Land Claim Agreement, the Umbrella Final Agreement and the Nunavut Land Claims Agreement. The Nunavut agreement was especially significant because it divided the Northwest Territories into two, creating the eastern jurisdiction of Nunavut, where Inuit language and culture is entrenched in public government. Under this agreement, the Inuit of Nunavut gave up their title to the land and water in exchange for self-government and a budget to pay for services and fee-simple land. Revenues from resource extraction like mining, oil, gas and other sources remain with the federal government. As per usual, in 2006 the Inuit of Nunavut filed a $1 billion lawsuit against the government, claiming it had already breached sixteen sections of the treaty in fundamental ways.

Even more contentious has been modern-day treaties in the Mackenzie Valley, where the Crown has ignored mostly all of its commitments in Treaties 8 and 11. The Gwich'in Tribal Council got tired of waiting for the government to man up and stop being a deadbeat dad, so in 1992 it surrendered all its Aboriginal claims, rights and titles to lands and waters anywhere within Canada. The agreement also includes a clause "to indemnify and forever save harmless" the Canadian government from all future Gwich'in actions, suits and claims of Crown liability. Yipes! Now that's what I call a done deal. In return the Gwich'in were to receive $75 million and "Gwich'in title," which included subsurface mineral rights. The Sahtu Dene along with the Metis in the Great Bear Lake region settled for a similar package two years later.

Despite the efforts of Aboriginal peoples to have their treaties recognized internationally, the Government of Canada insists the agreements are a matter of domestic law. The government's position was evident in 1993 and 1994 when the Canadian, US and Mexican governments instituted the North American Free Trade Agreement. This treaty-making process ignored Aboriginal delegations even though the new treaty was to be imposed on territories already subject to the terms and conditions of treaties with indigenous peoples. On January 1, 1994, the day the treaty came into effect, the anti-Aboriginal nature of NAFTA was greeted by an Indian uprising in Chiapas, Mexico.

On the other side of the coin, the election of the Parti Québécois in 1994 and sovereignty referendum in 1995 raised issues about who gains custody of the Indians if Quebec ever decides to divorce Canada. In a referendum, ninety-six percent of Cree people voted to stay with Canada if Quebec separates. The Quebec Inuit also held a referendum on the issue and produced similar results. Commenting on these polls, Assembly of First Nations Chief Matthew Coon Come (say that ten times real fast) warned that if Canada is divisible, then so is Quebec. He explained that Quebec as a province does not have the ability to negotiate a treaty with the Cree because only sovereigns have treaty-making power. Since Quebec is a province and not a state, treaty-making power rests exclusively between Canada and Aboriginal peoples.

In 1995, the government of Canada launched a new process called the Inherent Right to Self-Government Policy. The policy recognized that no one form of government would work for all

Aboriginal communities. Self-government arrangements would therefore take many forms based on historical, cultural, political and economic circumstances of a First Nations community.

Treaties and the Average Joe

With this brief survey of some of the major treaties in Canada's history, the question still remains of how these treaties affect the average Canadian. For many, there is a misconception that treaties were signed hundreds of years ago, only dealt with the issues of the day and no longer apply to the present reality of Canada. As a result, a commonly uttered statement is, "I wasn't around when the government stole the land, so why should I have to pay for it?" This statement is usually followed by, "Indians should get over it and move on." The problem with this argument is that Native people in Canada were not actually conquered, nor was their land stolen.

159

The rights of Native people today are a result of centuries of negotiation entrenched in legally binding contracts. The real problem is that the terms and obligations in these treaties have largely been ignored. If you examine the strategy of the Canadian government, you'll find that in many cases it is careful not to suggest that treaties are invalid or that Aboriginal sovereignty does not exist. That would be a lie. Instead, the government opts to tie up land and treaty claims in the court systems knowing that most Native communities are unable to sustain the cost of a lengthy legal battle. The hope seems to be that desperation and poverty will result in First Nations extinguishing their land title for a cash buyout, much the same way the Plains Indians did during the Numbered Treaties.

Nevertheless, as legal precedents roll in that favour Native claims, the federal government is extremely aware that something must be done where treaties have not been signed. As a result, it continues to exert pressure on First Nations communities with chronic underfunding and an excessive bureaucratic nightmare. Resource extraction and industrial projects are granted approval without the consent of the Aboriginal communities who suffer their effects. Bureaucrats continue to ignore the fact that many First Nations have undrinkable water systems. Housing shortages create social crises. Decades-long treaty and land claim processes drive communities into debt and make only a tiny elite group of administrators and lawyers filthy rich. In most cases, the government will allow these land or treaty claims to languish in court while using taxpayers' money to pay for legal costs.

Let me put it another way. Let's say you walk into McDonald's and order a Big Mac. You hand over your money and get a receipt. You now have an agreement that in exchange for your money you will receive a Big Mac. Five minutes goes by, then another five minutes, and before you know it you have been waiting over three centuries. Finally you approach the cashier and demand your delinquent Big Mac. The cashier asks to see your receipt, which you promptly display. He then informs you that you need to prove that the original intent of the receipt was a promise to provide you with a Big Mac. "After all, that receipt is from three centuries ago. It could have meant anything." To top it off, the other customers around you are receiving their Big Macs, no questions asked, and they're shouting at you: "Get over it and move on. Quit looking for free handouts!" So you take McDonald's to court and their lawyers are happy to stretch out the proceedings until you are flat broke because they know if you could actually afford a legal battle, you wouldn't be eating at McDonald's in the first place. And that, my friends, is how the land and treaty process works. It's all just lawyers, money and Big Macs.

In proving the underlying spirit and intent of the treaties, many valid questions have to be raised: What was the understanding of the various parties when they were formulating the bargains? How were the terms of the treaties interpreted or explained to Aboriginal people in their own languages? And how do the original terms apply within a modern context?

When interpreting and implementing a legal contract, the understanding of both parties is always taken into account. Treaties are no different in this respect. The majority of Aboriginal leaders who signed the treaty agreements understood them as a relationship of co-existence with the Crown and the sharing of land and resources. The Crown has continuously insisted that the treaties represented the complete surrender of Indian land in exchange for a small reserve and limited rights to hunt, fish and trap.

This tenuous claim that treaties were simple real estate deals where Natives agreed to sell valuable parcels of land for small lump-sum payments and small annual payments — usually $5 per treaty Indian per year — is ridiculous and falsely paints Aboriginal people as ignorant savages with no concept of land value or negotiating skills. Instead of admitting that the government might not be fulfilling its treaty obligations to Aboriginal people, the popular fallacy is that Indians willingly negotiated away lands and resources for a bunch of whisky and shiny beads. Hopefully, we've seen enough evidence to the contrary by now.

By the way, to address that shiny beads and trinkets point — the legend that Natives sold Manhattan to the Dutch for twenty-four dollars and beads and trinkets is a load of horse hooey. The story is much more complicated than that and in fact, the Indians the Dutch met on the Big Apple didn't even own Manhattan. They were just passing through as part of a co-existence agreement they had with the permanent Indian residents there (see, land *sharing*, that's what Indians negotiated back then). Historians believe that the Dutch actually gave the Indians a whole whack of really good stuff in exchange for Manhattan, which is irrelevant because the Indians just said, "Cool guys, thanks for the swag. Say 'hi' to the actual owners of this place for us when they show up. Laterz!" So technically, Manhattan like a large portion of Canada may be populated by millions of illegal non-Native squatters. But I digress…

Treaty Rights and Responsibilities

In 1990 the Supreme Court of Canada determined that "treaties and statutes relating to Indians should be liberally construed and uncertainties resolved in favour of the Indians." This ruling was based on a similar ruling in the US that stated Indian treaties "must therefore be construed, not according to the technical meaning of its words to learned lawyers, but in the sense in which they would naturally be understood by the Indians." As a result, there has been much care taken to ensure that modern-day treaties are not written using any language that could be misconstrued as surrender or extinguishment.

Another key aspect of the debate is the question of how the government of Canada could properly fulfill its fiduciary responsibility to Aboriginal people when its own Crown officials were signing legal documents outlining the extinguishment of Aboriginal rights. The Crown cannot uphold and protect Native rights while at the same time benefiting from the extinguishment of those rights; that's like putting the fox in charge of the henhouse. Were Crown officials in a conflict of interest when they dealt with Aboriginal peoples on this basis? More importantly, are the benefits and land acquired by the Crown through treaties even valid given the breach by Crown officials of their fiduciary obligations to Aboriginal peoples? (All these questions and more on the next episode of *As the World Turns*.)

Regardless of the endless debate, the original agreements still stand and the Royal Proclamation was reaffirmed in 1982 when Canada's constitution was repatriated. Since then, Aboriginal title has been upheld by the Supreme Court of Canada, which stated in 1997 that Canada's constitution "did not create Aboriginal rights; rather, it accorded constitutional status to those rights which were existing."

Among non-Native people there is widespread ignorance surrounding Canada's treaty obligations. Instead, they are taught to devalue indigenous nationhood and culture, and to try to force Indians to be just like them. After many decades of policies based on this assimilative sentiment, the Royal Commission on Aboriginal Peoples presented a five-volume report and hundreds of recommendations in 1996. In its summary the commissioners wrote:

163

> Canadians need to understand that Aboriginal peoples are nations. That is, they are political and cultural groups with values and lifeways distinct from those of other Canadians. They lived as nations — highly centralized, loosely federated, or small and clan-based — for thousands of years before the arrival of Europeans. As nations, they forged trade and military alliances among themselves and with the new arrivals. To this day, Aboriginal people's sense of confidence and well-being as individuals remains tied to the strength of their nations. Only as members of restored nations can they reach their potential in the twenty-first century.

The commission's twenty-year plan for changing the relationship with indigenous nations has been ignored for the last eighteen years.

Today, most people associate treaty rights with "special privileges" that set Aboriginals apart from mainstream society. In fact, the majority of non-Native Canadians also have treaty rights.

Thanks to treaties, Canadians can share the land, move about freely, engage in economic activity, govern themselves, and maintain their cultural and spiritual beliefs without fear of persecution. But instead of viewing treaties as agreements that enabled Canada to strengthen and grow into the financial and democratic power it is today, most Canadians view them as hindrances to progress that allow Native people to suckle at the teat of taxpayers and feast on the smorgasbord of free stuff. In the next chapter, we'll take a look at some of the specific misconceptions that Native people endure surrounding these so-called "special privileges" and "free stuff." So follow me on this journey, won't you? If you need a ride I can give you a lift in my free truck.

NÄTIVE LÄND

"Let's call ahead and make reservations"

WELCOME BACK. SO NOW WE'RE AWARE OF SOME OF the treaties that cover over half the Canadian land mass. The constant debate as to how the treaties' terms and conditions apply in a modern context is icky lawyer stuff that I'm not touching with a ten-foot totem pole. Instead, let's take a look at how treaties that were intended to ensure autonomous co-existence between Natives and Canada devolved into a system where First Nations became wards of the state. Our first stop on this journey: the British North America Act.

Remember the good ol' days when the Royal Proclamation of 1763 protected Indian land and traditional ways of life and all dealings with Indians went through the Crown? Things were so much simpler back then. We knew how things worked and there was at least an outward appearance of mutual respect. Well apparently that wasn't good enough for Britain when it decided to make Canada a big-boy, grown-up country. Ain't that always the case? Your friends start having kids and all of a sudden it's *adios* to their old pals the Indians.

To this day there is a lot of debate as to whether the Royal Proclamation recognizes or undermines Native sovereignty. Regardless, it does establish that Native people had certain rights to the land. It provides an argument that prevents the Crown from exercising sovereignty over First Nations and affirms Aboriginal self-determination in allocating those lands. The Royal Proclamation also outlined a policy to protect Aboriginal rights and in doing so recognized those rights existed. The Royal Proclamation is a fundamental document for First Nations land claims and self-government. It is the first legal recognition by the British Crown of Aboriginal rights and imposes a fiduciary duty of care on the Crown. It is therefore mentioned in section 25 of the Canadian Charter of Rights and Freedoms. Since the Royal Proclamation, Canada has gone through numerous changes to its governing charters and each time greater efforts are made to erode Native rights. The first of these major documents was the British North America Act of 1867, later known and herein referred to as the Constitution Act of 1867.

The Constitution Act of 1867

When Britain handed over governing authority to the new country of Canada, it was essentially just handing over administrative control. Canada was still a British colony but the Constitution Act enabled the governing body of Canada to create provinces and exercise control over resources and other domestic matters. Essentially, the governors of Canada were just middle managers like Bill Lumbergh in the movie *Office Space*: "Yeeaah... I'm going to need you to go ahead and come in on Monday to steal the Indians' land. Okay? That'd be great."

While the rest of Canada was being governed by its newly appointed bureaucrats, the treaty Indians still had a direct relationship with the Crown in England as established in the Royal Proclamation. After the War of 1812, Britain no longer relied on the Indians to protect the Canadian borders but was desperate for the lands that Natives had secured in the treaties. They were also desperate for lands not covered by treaties but were protected by the Royal Proclamation. These lands still had to be negotiated away from the Indians. So Britain got sneaky and decided to change the entire relationship with Natives through its new Constitution Act. As previously mentioned, section 91(24) of the Constitution Act stated that the federal government now had jurisdiction over "Indians, and the Lands reserved for the Indians." This jurisdiction was overseen by the federal department of Indian and Northern Affairs Canada (INAC), which has recently changed its name to Aboriginal Affairs and Northern Development Canada (AANDC).

The new Constitution Act ensured that the federal government was responsible for everything to do with Indians including lands, resources, education, etc. and that the provinces were supposed to keep their noses out of Indian business. The rest of Canada, however, was governed under the full authority of the Constitution Act, which split Canada into two levels of government: federal *and* provincial. Under sections 92A and 93 of the Constitution Act, non-renewable natural resources and education fell under the jurisdiction of the provinces. However, on Indian lands those two areas fell under the jurisdiction of the federal government. As the provinces gained more power, the federal government started allowing the provinces to deal with non-renewable resources on Indian lands as well. This did not sit well with the Indians who were all like, "Yo feds, why are the provinces all up in my grill?"

And the federal government was all like, "Ummm... What? Can't hear you."

And the Indians were all like, "This land is my land. You got your own land. This land was not made for you and me."

And the federal government was all like, "That's catchy. Someone should turn that into a song. I mean, what? Can't hear you."

And the Indians were all like, "The provinces can't touch our land unless we sell it to you. Once we do then you can build a waterslide or Pottery Barn or whatever white folks build. Until then keep your provinces on their side of the tracks or there's going to be a turf war, homie!"

And the federal government stuck its fingers in its ears, and was all like, "La la la, I can't hear you. La la la!"

For the record, I am well aware that my years of living in Los Angeles have not made me more adept at street vernacular. I apologize. Moving on...

By letting the provinces have free reign, the federal government was getting out of its fiduciary responsibility to protect "fraud and abuses" on Indian Land by allowing the provinces to commit the "fraud and abuses" on Indian Land. This was great for the provinces, who had no responsibility to the Indians and could grab as much Indian land as possible. Also, whichever province got the most Indian land won the sales conference and got a free set of steak knives (or something like that). This slippery manoeuvre has come back to bite the federal government in its right honourable buttocks many times over the years. It's also why so many land claims that actually make it to the Supreme Court tend to come out in favour of the Indians. Nice try, nineteenth-century federal government.

The federal government then attempted to further weasel its way out of its fiduciary responsibility by enacting a piece of legislation that codified the Indian rights established in the Royal Proclamation. Naturally, the Indians were not consulted on this new legislation, which came to be called (cue the scary music)...

The Indian Act!

The introduction of the Indian Act in 1876 flipped the Crown's responsibility of protecting the Indians from outside forces to essentially protecting the Indians from themselves. The government was still charged with looking after the best interests of the Indians, but through the Indian Act it could now decide what those best interests were. And what it thought was in the Indians' best interests was to turn them into wards of the state until they were ready to give up their traditional ways of life, become Christians, become farmers, get a white education, give up their land and rights, and assimilate into white culture.

At first the government believed that the Indians would gladly abandon their land and rights in exchange for the honour of becoming Canadian citizens. This delightful offer was called "enfranchisement," but the Indians were not very keen. When the Gradual Civilization Act passed in 1857, only one person voluntarily enfranchised. So the government got all huffy and made enfranchisement compulsory for all men of age twenty-one who could read and write English.

By 1869, the federal government created the Gradual Enfranchisement Act, which granted Indian Affairs extreme control over Status Indians such as determining who was of "good moral character" and other such nonsense. The Act also restricted the powers of governing band councils, controlled alcohol consumption and determined who could receive band and treaty benefits. It was also responsible for gender-based restrictions on becoming a Status Indian.

Sex and the Status

One of the biggest differences between Euro-Canadian and First Nations cultures in the nineteenth century was its treatment of women. In Native cultures, women were considered equals and often held great decision-making power in tribe affairs. In Euro-Canadian culture, women were considered the legal property of their husbands. When the Canadian government forced the Indian Act on Native communities, it included sexist legislation that ran contrary to many Native cultures. The most enduring of that legislation revolved around the status of Indian women.

Until 1985, the Indian Act stripped a woman and her children of Indian Status if she married a man without Indian Status. "Illegitimate" children of Status Indian women could also lose Status if the father was not a Status Indian and if the child's Status was "protested" by the Indian agent. Furthermore, if the mother and paternal grandmother did not have Status before marriage, their children could be stripped of their Status when they turned twenty-one. Much of this discrimination comes from amendments to the Indian Act in 1951. Although Indian women would lose their Status if they married a non-Status man, non-Status women would *gain* Indian Status if they married a Status man. This double standard further reinforced the Euro-Canadian notion of women as a man's property.

Government was looking for ways to force Indians into the dominant culture, and its most effective tool in accomplishing this goal was through the Indian Act. By not fulfilling treaty obligations and withholding Indian rights, the federal and provincial governments essentially used hostage techniques to starve out the Indians and usurp their bargaining power. The governments were then able to swoop in and establish Indian reserves.

The Indian Reserve System

As colonists moved west, the federal government capitalized on the poverty and desperation of Indians and was able to acquire vast amounts of land as seen in the Numbered Treaties. Many of these treaties stipulated that in exchange for surrendering land, the Indians would be placed on reserves and protected by the federal government. However, there were still a number of First Nations that did not sign treaties and continued to live on unceded land — particularly my people, the Indians of British Columbia (those rascally scamps). Since the Royal Proclamation prescribed that any land west of the boundary line (which had now moved west to British Columbia) must be negotiated with the Indians living there, surely the government immediately started negotiating land-surrender agreements with the BC Indians, right? Right?

Nope. Through a series of deceptions and strong-arm tactics, the federal government moved many BC First Nations onto reserves without any negotiations or land-surrender agreements. To this day, the majority of British Columbia is still on unceded Indian land, which has led to some of the largest and most comprehensive land claims in the country. It has also led to some huge logistical nightmares for present-day premiers in BC who must navigate the legacy of past governments' arrogance. Once again: nice try, nineteenth-century federal government.

To this day, you'll often hear Canadians say, "Settlement was inevitable. It was nice of the government to give free land to the Indians so they could live freely and untouched." Actually, settlement was not inevitable in Canada. In fact it could not even have occurred if Indians did not agree to surrender their land. The fact that the government used so many illegal, deceptive and inhumane tactics to acquire those lands is why there are so many land and treaty claims today. In cases where agreements were broken, the First Nations believe they are collecting on past debts. In cases where no agreements were made, the First Nations believe they are reclaiming land that the government had no right to allow Canadians to settle on in the first place. Whether you agree with the First Nations perspective or not, the Canadian courts have ruled on the side of Indians enough times to suggest there is validity in the First Nations' point of view. But I digress...

Anyway, once a First Nation agreed to give up portions of its territory for a smaller reserve, they were then placed under the control of the Department of Indian Affairs. The federal government held the reserve in trust for the Indians who were supposed to live there untouched, as a separate entity, and supported by government obligations such as housing, education, health care, etc. You know, the stuff that other Canadians get but when Indians get them they are called "special rights and privileges." Unfortunately, most reserve land was barren and undevelopable so the Indians came to rely more and more on government assistance. In other words, if North America was a turkey, reserve land would be the leftover bag of giblets that you discover once the turkey is cooked.

Under the Indian Act, non-Natives were forbidden to trespass on reserve land but there were some non-Natives who had carte blanche to enter the reserve and dictate every aspect of reserve life. These people were called *Indian agents* and they were charged with enforcing the provisions of the Indian Act that essentially relegated Native people to the status of children.

Indian Act "Special Rights and Privileges"

As amendments were made over the years, the Indian Act became more repressive and focused on the ultimate goal of extinguishing Native rights. However, many Canadians believe the Indian Act actually gave special rights and privileges to First Nations. In this section I'll touch on just a few of the realities of those so-called "special rights and privileges."

In 1881 officers of the Indian Department, including Indian agents, were given the power of justices of the peace, then the next year of magistrates. Even if the officers had never practised law, they still became judge, jury and legal counsel wrapped into one. *Indian privilege #1: Reserve Indians did not have the same due legal process that other Canadians enjoyed.*

Another amendment in 1881 prohibited Indians in the prairie provinces from selling agricultural goods without a permit from an Indian agent. In most cases, if the agriculture produced by the Indians competed with non-Native farmers, the Indian agent would not grant permission for the Indians to sell their produce off-reserve. *Indian Privilege #2: Indians were not allowed equal opportunity to participate in trade and commerce even if they wanted to.* Many Canadians today will notice a lack of Indian businesses and say, "My great-grandparents came to this country with nothing and built a business. Why couldn't the Indians?" My response is, "Was it legal for your great-grandparents to start a business and sell freely to other Canadians? Cool. It wasn't legal for mine. Congratulations on your great-grandfather's dry-cleaning empire. You can thank the Canadian government for eliminating Indians as a source of competition."

And remember in the treaties how Indians insisted on schools for their newly formed reserves? For some reason, many non-Natives believe Indians were opposed to education. This makes little

173

sense when you consider the history of Indians incorporating and adapting European culture into their own. First Nations understood that their survival relied on learning European ways so they could better understand the encroaching culture. The difference is they wanted schools to strengthen their culture, not extinguish it. The Canadian government used education to abolish Native culture in the enfranchisement acts and later through the Indian residential schools.

While the residential schools' primary goal was to convert Native children to Christianity and "civilize them," they also forced them to learn agriculture to ensure they would not go back to their traditional ways of hunting and fishing after graduation. The Gradual Civilization Act awarded fifty acres of land to any Indian male deemed "sufficiently advanced in the elementary branches of education" and would automatically "enfranchise" him, removing any tribal affiliation or treaty rights. Even though these schools were designed to enfranchise Indians, they mostly trained them for menial labour and not for entrance into post-secondary education. *Indian Privilege #3: Indians received substandard education designed to erase their culture and language and left them unprepared to gain employment in the dominant culture.* The students endured epidemic proportions of violence, molestation, sickness and often death in these schools.

In 1884 the Indian Act prohibited religious ceremonies and dances, then in 1895 *criminalized* many Aboriginal ceremonies, resulting in the conviction of numerous Aboriginal people for practising their religions. Between 1900 and 1904, approximately fifty Aboriginal people were arrested and twenty were convicted for participating in dances and ceremonies. *Indian Privilege #4: Indians were denied freedom of religion, one of the few peoples in Canadian history denied this fundamental right.*

Then in 1905, an amendment allowed for the removal of

Aboriginals from reserves near towns with more than eight thousand residents. So if your town was big enough that it warranted building a McDonald's but there wasn't enough space for the drive-thru, you didn't need to worry! Remember those Indians on protected lands that were to remain untouched? We can move them now! Maybe we'll give them an Egg McMuffin for their troubles. *Indian Privilege #5: Indians living on protected Indian Lands were only protected as long as they weren't close enough to peek over the fence at white people; then—like laundry day—it was time to separate the whites from the colours.*

The next year of annual Indian Act amendments entitled band **175** members to receive fifty percent of the sale price of reserve lands following the surrender of that land. Well, if that isn't impetus for poverty-stricken, desperate Indians to give up their constitutional protection and start selling off land to the government, then I don't know what is. *Indian Privilege #6: Constitutionally binding land agreements could be dismissed if the government could convince the Indians to sell at rock-bottom, Columbus Day sale prices.* Oops, I mentioned his name again. I guess I have to put a dollar in the swear jar. Land rights were undercut further through the Oliver Act of 1911, allowing municipalities and companies to seize unsurrendered portions of reserve land if they needed it for roads, railways and other public works. Another provision allowed a judge to move an entire reserve away from a municipality if it was deemed "expedient." *Indian privilege # 7: In addition to just moving people, now your entire reserve could be moved as long as there was an equal or lesser quality piece of crappy land waiting for you.*

A 1914 amendment required Indians to get official permission before appearing in "Aboriginal costume" in any "dance, show, exhibition, stampede or pageant." Permission was rarely given because dressing in traditional regalia was akin to practising Native religion, which was illegal. The only time permission might have been given was if visiting dignitaries came to Canada and the government wanted to parade out their "noble Indians." Hey, just like the Olympics! *Indian Privilege #8: White people could dress up like Indians on Halloween or any other time of the year, but real Indians couldn't dress up like Indians ever.*

In 1918 the superintendent-general of Indian Affairs was granted authority to lease out uncultivated reserve lands to non-Natives if the new leaseholder wanted to use it for farming... Whoa, wait! Now non-Natives could use Indian land? I guess they're not technically *buying* it but still... Also, non-Natives that leased Indian land for farming or pasture didn't have to worry about competition from Indian farmers because — well, you know — permission from the Indian agent and all that. Sigh. *Indian Privilege #9: Indian land wasn't really Indian land as long as a non-Native had good credit and could lease. Back then it was easier for a white man to lease Indian land than it was for me to get a lease on my Toyota Yaris.*

A new amendment in 1927 prevented anyone, Aboriginal or otherwise, from accepting money for Indian legal claims without a special licence from the superintendent-general, preventing any First Nation from pursuing Aboriginal land claims. *Indian Privilege #10: You know how the law says Canadians are entitled to hire lawyers and have their cases heard in courts of law, in front of juries of their... You know what, let's just stop there — Indians couldn't even hire a lawyer. Case closed.* This law highlights just how important snatching up Indian land really was to the Canadian government.

As an example of how prescriptive and discriminatory the Indian Act amendments became, in 1930 pool hall owners were prevented from allowing entrance to any Indian who "by inordinate frequenting of a pool room either on or off an Indian reserve misspends or wastes his time or means to the detriment of himself, his family or household." This law further enforced the already illegal act of serving alcohol to Indians, even off-reserve. The owner could be fined or even be sent to jail for a month. (This amendment obviously didn't achieve its goal because I have lost an inordinate amount of money to Native pool hustlers in many pool halls over the years.) *Indian Privilege #11: Indians would be spared the staining of blue chalk on their fingers, but at least they would be spending more time back on their reserve which may or may not still be there when they got home.*

In 1936 Indian agents were empowered to direct band council **177** meetings and to cast a deciding vote in the event of a tie. *Indian Privilege #12: Even with the incredible lack of autonomy in Indian communities, Indians weren't even allowed to discuss and vote on issues without the Indian agent determining what could be discussed and how. As far as the deciding vote being cast by the Indian agent—as we all know from baseball the tie always goes to the runner and on Indian reserves the runner was always the federal government.*

SO HOW ARE YOU LIKING ALL THE PREFERENTIAL TREAT-ment and special privileges for Indians? While Canadians enjoyed the right to vote, move freely around the country, start a business, own property, have it protected by law and do pretty much anything they wanted within reason, Indian Reserves were a sort of Bizarro World where the exact opposite occurred. The only way Indians could enjoy the rights and freedoms of regular Canadians would be to—you got it—enfranchise! Pretty clever nineteenth-century federal government but once again, nice try.

There is another misconception that while these laws were being imposed on reserves, the Indians were just sitting idly by and allowing it to happen. This fits nicely into the Euro-Canadian idea of Indians as a vanishing race. Nowadays, right-leaning folks say Indians are living in a victim mentality. While this is certainly true of some Native people, as it is for some non-Native people, the First Nations legacy is far from being one of victimization. Many Native leaders were fighting like hell against these restrictive laws, sometimes at their own legal and physical costs. Even back then, Native leaders understood that the government was in breach of its legal and constitutional obligations, and they weren't going anywhere until those obligations were rightfully fulfilled, dammit! Whoa, I just had a militant moment there. Excuse me for a moment while I change out of my headband and camouflage fatigues. Talk amongst yourselves.

Modern-day Reserves

So even if the reserves of yore existed as the complete opposite of their supposed intent, you're probably saying to yourself, "Yeah, yeah, yeah, but that was then, this is now. Today, Indian reserves are island paradises where chiefs live in mansions, everyone owns a fleet of Lamborghinis and Indians lie around all day being fanned with palm leaves and fed grapes by eunuchs. I know this because I read it in a *Sun* newspaper" (which is a total lie because no one actually *reads* the *Sun* newspapers; they just skim through the articles on their way to the Sunshine Girl). But yes, since the 1880s and early 1900s, things have improved on reserves. Moderately. At the end of the Second World War, human rights violations left an indelible mark on the citizens of Canada, who gained a greater awareness of the plight of Indians on reserves. This new-found awareness resulted in further amendments to the Indian Act that began to restore the basic human rights denied to Native people for far too long.

In 1951, new amendments allowed the vote in band elections

for Status women, the free pursuit of land claims and the practice of religious ceremonies. However, the Act also made enfranchisement mandatory for First Nations women who married non-Status men, which resulted in the loss of Status for themselves and for any children from that marriage. In 1961, the compulsory enfranchisement of men or bands was also removed from the Indian Act.

Then in the 1980s all sorts of exciting things happened for Indians, and I'm not just referring to acid-washed denim. In 1985 the Indian Act was amended so that First Nations women could regain their Status even after "marrying out." Their children could also be granted Status but not their grandchildren. This amendment was an improvement to the previous gender-based Status laws but it still fed the government's goal of extinguishing all Status rights by essentially breeding Status out of the Indian population. Unless every Status Indian marries only other Status Indians until the end of time, Native Status will be gone before we know it. Today, around half of all Status Indians marry non-Status people, which should accomplish complete legal assimilation in the matter of a few generations.

In 2011, the Indian Act was amended again so that grandchildren of women who lost their Status as a result of marrying non-Status men became entitled to Indian status. Since then, approximately forty-five thousand people became entitled to register for Status. The impact of this new wave of eligible Status Indians is yet to be determined, but with more of them around to marry it might take a little longer for that two-generation cut-off to take effect. I never get tired of saying this: Nice try, nineteenth-century federal government. Obviously there are a lot more amendments to the Indian Act than the ones listed here. So if you want to know more I would recommend sitting down and perusing the entire Act. It makes great bathroom reading.

Land Title

Today, reserves that are not subject to the terms of modern-day treaties and/or other negotiated agreements are still under control of the Indian Act; reserve land is still held in trust by the federal government, who has authoritative control. Under the Indian Act, Indians still do not own private property on reserves since Aboriginal title is a communal right. Also, the land can still be sold only to the federal government. On the plus side, Aboriginal title is protected by the Canadian Constitution.

There are some who believe that by moving onto Indian reserves, First Nations gave up their right to land title by default. I don't know where they get these "facts" but the Supreme Court of Canada would beg to differ. In 1997, the landmark Delgamuukw decision finally clarified that Aboriginal title to most of the land in British Columbia had never been extinguished, even under Canadian law. This ruling essentially recognized that large areas across the country had never been legally acquired by the Crown through treaties. In 1999, the Supreme Court passed down another judgment confirming that the Peace and Friendship Treaties of 1760–61 did not cede land or resources either. The implications of these decisions may be lost on many Canadians who may have to contend with the fact that much of the land the government gave them to settle on was never the government's to give. Aaaaawkkkwaard!

For centuries many First Nations have been plunged so deeply into poverty that title to their land was the only bargaining chip they had left. Today, some First Nations are fed up with negotiating and are buying back their land as an alternative to the lengthy and frustrating judicial system. Unfortunately much of the land in remote areas holds no real estate value, and the people there exist in an economic vacuum. Indian Bands that have succeeded in large-scale development, as well as opening businesses and financial institutions, are generally close to urban areas. With the success of these businesses the discussion has shifted to privatizing Indian land. There is a concern that privatization would open up First Nations to governments and private land developers who will swoop in and do away with First Nations title and rights. History would tend to agree.

In 1934 the US government passed the Indian Reorganization Act, which allowed Native Americans to privatize resources on Indian lands. This led to the breakup of reservations and increased poverty for American Indians. Similarly, prior to signing NAFTA in 1994 the Mexican government changed its constitution to remove protection of communally held lands, called *ejidos*, and allow for privatization. Once this protection was gone, communities began losing their lands to wealthy landowners and transnational corporations through violence and fraud. Canadian Aboriginals have argued that the privatization of their lands would likely have similar results. On the other hand, there are some who believe that privatization is the only way to free First Nations from the regime of the Indian Act.

In some instances, Canadian First Nations lease portions of their land to developers or resource extraction companies in exchange for mining rights or oil revenues. Sometimes they'll lease a portion of land just for the rent money. All of these deals must first go through the federal government who often facilitates the terms and conditions of the agreements. Land negotiation in exchange for compensation occurs every day in the public and private sector of Canada and is the basis of all real-estate and business transactions. Yet for some reason there is a perception that Natives are getting "special treatment" or "privileges" for participating in the free-market economy the way any average Canadian might. It would appear that some would still prefer to have an Indian agent determine when and to whom an Indian can sell their produce. On the flip side, there are others who believe this whole Indian land mess could be avoided if all land was just communal and title didn't exist (once again I say, "Get a haircut, damn hippie!").

Free Housing

Another misconception that reserves are a freeloader's paradise stems from the myth that Aboriginals get "free housing." This myth is so overblown that many people believe no matter where an Indian lives, be it on a reserve or in Toronto, Aboriginals have their houses paid for. If that's the case then I want to know where all this free money was when I was struggling to make my Toronto mortgage payments. In order to shed some light on this "free housing" myth we have to go back to the definition of "Aboriginal" as stated in the constitution: First Nations, Inuit and Metis. As of the 2011 census there were 1,400,685 Aboriginal people in Canada, which breaks down into 59,445 Inuit; 451,795 Metis and 851,560 First Nations (Status and non-Status). As previously mentioned, so-called "Native privileges" only really apply to registered (Status) First Nations living on-reserve. Inuit and Metis people don't have reserves so they are out of this equation. First Nations people (Status and non-Status) that live off-reserve also have to buy their own houses, pay property taxes, and deal with their neighbours' bratty kids and barking dogs just like every other Canadian. As of 2011, over half of all First Nations people with registered Indian status were living off-reserve, leaving us just over 300,000 people who are eligible for so-called "free houses." There are two types of housing that exist on-reserve: market housing and non-profit social housing.

Market housing is not free housing. It is the opposite of free housing. This is regular-people housing, like the house that Mr. and

Mrs. Smith live in at the end of Cherry Blossom Lane in suburban Canada. As of 2006, market-based home ownership rates on reserves were thirty-one percent, compared to sixty-nine percent among off-reserve Canadians. Did you catch that? About thirty-one percent of all houses on-reserve are bought or rented through Natives' own money. Not tax money—their own money. So even though home ownership rates are lower on-reserve, the notion that home ownership does not exist at all on reserves is a complete fallacy.

There are several problems with market housing on-reserve. For one, the land is held communally and cannot be split into individual properties. Therefore, homeowners do not technically own the property their houses sit on. The Indian Act also restricts the seizure of personal property on-reserve, which makes it difficult to secure a loan, since banks or lenders often require collateral that they can seize if the borrower defaults. To assist on-reserve borrowers, AANDC sometimes provides ministerial loan guarantees, meaning the band will act as a kind of co-signer for a loan and is ultimately responsible for paying it back if the borrower defaults. Not all communities can afford a default so loan guarantees are hard to come by. Lack of income is another major difficulty in purchasing market housing on-reserve, which brings us to social housing.

The Canadian Mortgage and Housing Corporation (CMHC) provides affordable housing to *all* Canadians in need regardless of whether they live on a reserve or not. The CMHC pays for close to 600,000 Canadians who have shelter and social housing needs. Non-profit social housing across the country is built through subsidies under section 95 of the National Housing Act. On-reserve housing is often called band housing, which is basically the same kind of non-profit housing available to all low-income Canadians. As of 2006, fifty-seven percent of on-reserve people lived in non-profit social housing.

Band housing is built with the help of government subsidies in the same way that social housing is built for all needy Canadians. In situations where First Nations people need help to pay their rent, AANDC provides social assistance just as the Canadian government does for other Canadians. Yes, you read that correctly, even on many reserves where social housing is light years behind the national standard, the people living in these substandard homes are paying rent. Hmmm, market-based housing on-reserve, paying rent for band housing... This whole "free housing" myth is getting less and less free as we go on.

184

Social housing on-reserve is no more "free" than social housing provided to Canadians off-reserve. But for those who still believe impoverished Natives shouldn't be provided with affordable shelter, it's your lucky day. In 2012 the CMHC cut funding for on-reserve housing by thirty percent. This cut is going to hurt the majority of reserves that are already grossly underfunded, despite the rumour that all reserves are gated communities teeming with mansions.

Indian Housing Realities

Even though reserves are supposed to receive the same quality of social housing as the rest of Canada, the reality is that reserves do not receive even close to the same level of support. In fact, many Native communities are quite literally wallowing in Third World conditions. Federal evaluations of First Nations housing have concluded that housing shortages on reserves are severe and only getting worse. According to a 2011 report, twenty thousand to thirty-five thousand new units need to be built just to keep up with current demand. The Assembly of First Nations estimates that it's even higher at eighty-five thousand units. On-reserve housing is substandard in almost every way, especially when you consider that forty-two percent of homes on reserves need major repairs, compared with seven percent in homes off reserves. Rates of overcrowding are six times greater on-reserve. In many communities you can find up to twenty people living in one tiny home — not by choice but by necessity. In some communities, the overcrowding is so severe that people sleep in shifts. It is not uncommon to see residents wandering their communities in below-freezing temperatures until it is their turn to sleep.

People in the mainstream constantly question where all the money goes for on-reserve housing. When they learn that AANDC supplies a lump sum to each reserve and leaves it up to the band council to allocate the funds, the first assumption is often that the chief and council are pocketing the money. What is constantly omitted is that in many communities the demand outweighs current funding levels. Housing on reserves deteriorates much faster, largely because of overcrowding but also because of poor construction and housing designs that don't match environmental realities. A common complaint is that many of the contractors Native communities are able to afford come into reserves and are not very concerned about the quality of the housing. Either that, or the reserve is only able to afford the bare minimum in building materials.

Maintenance is also a huge problem. The 2011 housing report inspected eighty homes, and determined that nearly every one needed repairs. Perhaps that's why less than thirty percent of the homes on-reserve that need repairs are getting them. Many communities are not close to building supply stores and in some isolated communities they have to bring in supplies by air, which adds a strain on already limited finances. In addition, substandard education and a lack of postsecondary opportunities means there are not a lot of people in the communities who are certified to build homes to code.

Bank Mortgages

As mentioned before, low income also prevents people from making investments in their homes. According to the 2006 census, the median annual income on reserves is $14,000, which means that the number of people with financial means to buy new homes is very small. Also, because homeowners on reserves can't own the property their houses are on, they must have their mortgages guaranteed by AANDC, which can take up to a year or more to process. With numerous problems surrounding loans on reserves and cash-strapped communities acting as insurers, band administrators must stretch the money they get from the federal government to cover repairs and build new housing. In most cases they can rarely afford to do both and often have to choose between fixing up rundown houses or building new ones to ease shortages.

The government spends an average of $272 million a year on First Nations housing and added an additional $400 million on an annual basis through the 2009 economic stimulus plan, but the federal housing evaluation concluded that it's not enough. Remember, these are not greedy chiefs and councils looking for some extra pocket change; rather, these are officials of the federal government who have confirmed a Native housing crisis. Still, many Canadians insist that if Native people just bought homes like "regular Canadians" they would have more pride and do whatever it takes to fix them up, no excuses. While there is certainly evidence that Native people who own homes on-reserve tend to be more emotionally invested in them, the reality is that on-reserve housing in its current state is not comparable to the benefits of home ownership for "regular Canadians." For one thing, "ownership" of a home on a reserve is a misnomer since the home buyer doesn't actually own the property. For another, the current financial state of the average on-reserve Native puts him or her way behind the "regular Canadian" who can afford a home and make repairs.

First Nations are often faced with hostility about the social housing they live in. More Canadians need to realize that social housing is not a Native right, it is a Canadian right—a right that is provided to all Canadians through the contribution of both Native *and* non-Native taxpayers. Wait a sec, did I just say "Native" and "taxpayers" in the same sentence? I can assume from all the teeth-gnashing that I did. In that case, this is probably a good point to segue into the most annoying and derisive of all the Native stereotypes.

Indian Taxes

The stereotype that frequently gets Canadian mouths foaming is that Aboriginals don't pay taxes. Those who subscribe to this misconception also tend to believe that Aboriginals who access housing and other social programs are unfairly benefiting from tax funds they are not contributing to. For example, the Frontier Centre for Public Policy printed an article that said, "Tax relief and tax reform must be based on the principle of fairness. Taxes should be based on income; meaning if people do not pay taxes, it should be because they are too poor to pay, not because of their ancestry." The Canadian Taxpayers Federation is a little more to the point: "Income—not race or ancestry—is the only valid basis for a tax exemption."

I actually agree with these statements. Race or ancestry should not be a basis for tax exemption. However, exemption from taxes negotiated in legally binding nation-to-nation agreements and entrenched in federal policy *is* a pretty good basis for tax exemption. As with the majority of Native issues, Native tax exemption is a matter of legal and constitutional precedent, not race, despite how loud the right wing love to scream about the tax-exempt Indian boogeyman. Hopefully by now we have seen enough examples of why Indian lands are not taxed. Indian lands were supposed to be protected by the government and taxing those lands might erode away the land base. However, for most Canadians the question is not why Indian lands are tax free but rather should they be taxed? Before we tackle this subject, it's important to note that revenue from land acquired from Indians, in exchange for the reserves they now languish on, has more than made up for lost revenue due to First Nations tax exemption.

As mentioned before I am a Status Indian, which means I have a Status card. Many of my non-Native friends believe this card is my "get out of taxes free" card. I cannot tell you the amount of times they've said, "Man, I gotta take you shopping with me. We can get so much tax-free stuff." Hmmm, I wonder if that's why I have so many non-Native friends. You cannot imagine the defeated look on their faces when I explain that my Status card is not an all-access pass to the tax-free VIP room. For the purposes of the following explanation, I'm going to take my Status card out of my wallet and demonstrate when and where I can use it and when and where I can't. I have a feeling by the time I am done I may have a few less non-Native friends.

So how much is actually lost in tax revenues every year due to privileged tax-free Indians? Before I can answer that, let's take a look at the official policy on Indian tax exemption. To quote AANDC:

> In general, Aboriginal people in Canada are required to pay taxes on the same basis as other people in Canada, except where the limited exemption under section 87 of the Indian Act applies. Section 87 says that the "personal property of an Indian or a band situated on a reserve" is tax exempt.

Wait, "limited exemption"? That can't be right! If you read the comments section on any online article about Natives (and unfortunately I do read them), you'll see that every single Native in Canada is sponging off the hard-earned tax dollars of benevolent Canadians. And if you believe everything you read on the internet I'd love to introduce you to a Nigerian prince who needs your help in getting his money from an offshore account.

For the record, this tax exemption has existed since before Confederation. When the Indians were negotiating away their land, the tax exemption was included as part of securing an autonomous land base for Native people. Ever since Confederation the Supreme Court of Canada has continuously affirmed that this exemption is designed to protect reserve land and property and not to bring economic benefits to Aboriginal people. Of course many Canadians will stomp their feet and scream, "How could that not benefit Natives? I work my ass off and they don't contribute anything!" Hold on there Mr. and Mrs. Misinformed, no need to yell. Remember your blood pressure.

189

Let's go back to section 87 of the Indian Act which says "personal property of an Indian or a band situated on a reserve" is tax exempt. The key words in that statement are "on a reserve." Keep that in mind as we go back to the 2011 census figure of 1,400,685 Aboriginals in Canada: First Nations, Metis and Inuit. Section 87 states that personal property of an "Indian or a band situated on a reserve" is tax exempt. If you recall, the Metis and Inuit are not Indians and do not have reserves so they are not subject to this tax exemption. Fare thee well fellow Aboriginals and say hello to Revenue Canada for us First Nations, will ya?

That leaves only First Nations (Status and non-Status) who are tax exempt. If you remember from Chapter 1, only Status (registered) Indians are considered "Indians" under the Indian Act so only Status Indians are eligible for tax exemption. So long non-Status Indians, give our regards to the Metis and Inuit in the

Revenue Canada lineup. (And while you're there say hi to all those irate Canadians who believe *all* Aboriginals are tax exempt.)

That leaves only Status Indians who are eligible for tax exemption. Hold on, we forgot about those three magic words in section 87: "on a reserve." It just so happens that over half of all Status Indians in Canada live off-reserve, which means they live closer to their nearest Revenue Canada office where they can pay their taxes alongside their non-Status, Metis and Inuit brethren. For the record, I am one of these Status Indians who no longer lives on a reserve and therefore has a long history of paying taxes. Lots and lots of taxes. You're welcome, Canada.

So that means in 2011 only about 314,366 Status Indians were living on-reserve and were eligible for tax exemption. If you factor in population increases since 2011 and different statistics based on varied accounting methods, we can assume that over 300,000 Indians are eligible for tax exemption. Oh, heck let's be even more liberal and round that number up even more so nobody's mouth gets frothy. Let's say that roughly 400,000 Indians are eligible for tax exemption. That's still way higher than the actual amount but what the hell...

But wait, there's more! In 2011, about twenty-eight percent of the Status Indian population was aged 0–14, which significantly decreases the population of eligible First Nations taxpayers. And the number of tax-exempt reserve Indians is even lower because a number of First Nations have included taxation policies in their self-governing agreements. More than 150 First Nations communities across Canada have their own property tax regime, which brings in over $76 million in revenues every year. The taxes are collected by the bands and used for the bands. There are also communities that have negotiated tax regimes with the federal government and collect taxes like the First Nations Sales Tax, the First Nations Goods and Services Tax and/or the First Nations Personal

Income Tax. In the Yukon, eleven out of the fourteen First Nations are no longer tax exempt under self-governing agreements.

Presto! We have just gone from all Aboriginals don't pay taxes to a pretty small percentage of the Aboriginal population that is tax exempt. That still leaves those Status Indians on reserves, not subject to Native tax regimes, who don't pay any taxes at all. Screw them, right? Well, even those on-reserve Status Indians are going to pay some taxes eventually. As a wise man once said, "The only two certainties in life are death and taxes." That goes for everyone, Native and non-Native. We'll get to that, but first we need to look at the specifics of how reserve tax exemption works and examine the limitations. Yes people, there *are* limitations.

Sales Tax

On-reserve tax exemption applies to both federal and provincial taxes. Status Indians who don't live on-reserve are not eligible for this tax exemption, unless they purchase goods and services *on-reserve* or are employed *on-reserve*. For example, I am a Status Indian but I no longer live on a reserve. However, if I shop at a Best Buy that is located on a reserve and purchase a flat screen TV, I can flash my Status card and I will be exempt from the sales tax. This is the scenario that makes me popular with my non-Native friends who want me to go shopping with them for big-ticket items. The only problem is you first have to find a reserve that is close enough to an urban centre and is financially capable of having a store that sells something other than fireworks or tobacco products. By the way, my Status card also allows me to purchase tobacco on-reserve tax-free, which is handy because nowadays cigarettes in Canada cost about as much as a flat screen TV.

Secondly, only goods that are purchased off-reserve and are delivered to the reserve by the retailer's *official agent* are tax exempt. This means that a Status Indian cannot buy a car in Toronto, drive it to the reserve and say it was shipped. The car would have to have been delivered by the car dealership or driven there by an agent of the car dealership. This would never happen. How many salesmen are going to drive a car to a reserve and then rely on the Indian who bought it to give them a ride back to town? In some provinces, goods must also be registered to a reserve address to be tax exempt. In most cases, the cost of delivery makes the tax savings negligible. Off-reserve dining, entertainment and other things that cannot be physically shipped to a reserve are also not tax exempt.

Now some of you might have noticed when you were standing in line at Future Shop that the Native family in front of you flashed their Status card and got the sales tax taken off the XBox they were paying for. Good catch. When I lived in Toronto, many shops in that city allowed point-of-purchase tax exemption even though I lived in the city and my goods were not shipped to a reserve. This is not a national policy and there are many cities in Canada where my Status card means absolutely nothing at the point of sale. Toronto on the other hand has some weird historical issues with treaties and questions as to whether or not it is technically Indian land, but let's not go there right now. Instead I'll just say that this off-reserve tax exemption is a result of a combination of individual provincial laws, agreements with Revenue Canada and store policy.

It's important to note that all of these policies have been put in place by the federal and provincial governments as well as individual businesses. If you don't like these policies you can protest to your elected officials or the businesses that implemented them. You cannot, however, accuse Indians of cheating the system without looking like a complete ignoramus or an internet troll. That said, the sales tax issue can be confusing. Many salespeople do not understand the exemption and some First Nations people aren't totally clear on it either. Regardless, it's only human for Indians to take advantage of policies that might ease their tax burden a little as long as they're not breaking any laws. Every Canadian does it! Don't believe me, just look at your receipts. Are you really going to tell me you're writing off that lunch at Hooters because you were "entertaining clients"? Come on... I mean really, come on!

Income Tax

Income is considered "personal property" if it's earned on-reserve. However, the Canadian courts have ruled that income must follow a series of "connecting factors" that link income to the reserve. The location of the duties and the residence of both the employee and employer must be considered to determine whether the income is tax exempt. Once you work off-reserve you have to pay income taxes, even if your employer is situated on a reserve and/or you live on a reserve.

For example, in addition to being a writer I am also an actor. How good or bad I am at either one of these things is irrelevant for this example. If I am cast in a play that is performed on a reserve, the income I earn is tax-exempt because I am a Status Indian. However, if I am cast in a summer stock production of *Our Town* that is being performed off the reserve, my income is taxable. It doesn't matter if my primary residence is on a reserve or not. By the way, if any producers are reading this and they happen to be mounting a production of *Our Town*, I am currently available to audition. Just sayin'.

There are some exceptions to these tax rules (aren't there always?), especially as it pertains to "services." Services provided on-reserve are tax exempt. Services provided off-reserve are not tax exempt, unless the services are purchased with "band money" for things like off-reserve consultants, lawyers, accountants, investment advisors, etc. and are used in the service of the reserve. This very limited exemption is because Indian monies are still considered the personal property of the Indian band situated on the reserve.

But what about corporations, you might ask? Even if you don't ask, I'm going to tell you anyway. First Nations corporations and trusts are not tax exempt because legally a corporation is a separate "legal person" and is therefore not an "Indian." So let's say an Indian Band forms the XYZ Logging Company on its reserve. Since XYZ Logging is not an Indian person or an Indian band, that corporation is subject to be taxed just like any other corporation in Canada, even if the corporation is 100% owned and operated by Indians. In addition, as long as XYZ's assets are owned by the corporation and not an Indian or an Indian band, then creditors can seize those corporate assets. That's right, even if the XYZ Corporation is on-reserve and is one hundred percent owned by Indians! Betcha didn't know that.

This begs the question, why would Indians form corporations on-reserve if their assets can be seized and their profits taxed? Well, remember how difficult it was to get a loan for a house on-reserve? The same goes for a business on-reserve. Banks generally won't give loans to an on-reserve business because they wouldn't be able to seize assets if the business defaults on the loan. But since XYZ Logging is a corporation, the banks are more than welcome to traipse onto the reserve and take back their sawmills, chainsaws, flannel shirts or whatever assets logging corporations have.

That still leaves the personal property of individual Indians on-reserve and the whole "unfairness" issue of not being able to seize or tax their property. There are many Canadians who believe that Indian reserves are like Cayman Island accounts where

Indians can stash all their money and property and be completely safe from seizure or taxation. Kind of like how the Duke boys are always safe from arrest once they make it across the Hazzard County line. This misconception leads to the fear that an Indian can put a down payment on a truck, drive it to the reserve and never has to make another payment on it ever again. (Hey! Maybe that's where that free truck myth comes in. Now it makes sense.) This is not even close to being true and only promotes mistrust between off-reserve businesses and Native customers.

What many don't realize is that the Indian Act also protects unpaid non-Native business owners in transactions with Indian customers. If an Indian has full ownership of his truck (bought it outright, fully paid off his car loan, etc.) then that truck cannot be seized as part of a bankruptcy, or whatever, as long as it remains on-reserve. However, if that Indian is leasing the truck or defaults on his car payments, then technically that truck still belongs to the bank or car dealership. Since the truck is not fully paid for and is not technically the personal property of the Indian, the vendor can get a sheriff to go to the reserve and repossess the hell out of that truck! Same with any other property that is not technically owned outright by the Indian, including TVs, furniture, juicers or whatever. Just like — say it with me, folks — every other Canadian!

OKAY, SO IT'S TRUE THAT A SMALL PORTION OF THE Aboriginal population receives limited tax exemptions and reserve protection under certain circumstances, but it's not even close to the anger-inducing stereotype that *all* Aboriginals are tax exempt. Incidentally, you might have noticed that I use the word "eligible" quite often when referring to Native tax exemption. This is because the majority of reserve Indians, although eligible, can't take advantage of exemptions even if they wanted to. The most

195

overlooked point in this whole issue is the fact that in order for one to be exempt from income tax, one must first earn an income: the unemployment rate for Aboriginal people is more than twice the national average.

Stereotypes have led to a perception that the reason for high unemployment on reserves is because Indians live so comfortably off tax dollars that they have no motivation to find a job. I wish the simple problem was that there were many jobs but Indians prefer to sponge off the tax dollars being heaped on them. That's a problem that could easily be rectified, so I really wish it were the case. (I also really wish that the entire Kardashian family would suddenly become allergic to TV cameras, but neither of these scenarios is going to happen any time soon.) Figures from the 2006 census tell us that First Nations living on reserves had an employment rate of fifty-two percent. Statistics Canada has not made average income numbers for on-reserve employment available but estimates place the median income level at $14,000. Yeah, not exactly swimming in cash.

More importantly, the tax exemption doesn't even come close to making up for the lack of funding that is supposed to go to First Nations. A 2011 report by the Assembly of First Nations states that in 2010, per capita federal funding for First Nations was $8,750. That's far lower than the $18,724 per capita spent by all three levels of government on non-indigenous Canadians. Stirring up false anger about Native tax policy is one of the many ways in which the federal government creates a backlash against inherent Native rights.

The most insulting aspect of the whole "Aboriginals don't pay taxes" myth is the fact that the majority of Aboriginal people pay their fair share of taxes just like every other Canadian. Yet these taxpaying Aboriginals must constantly endure accusations that they are freeloading leeches. What's more, the tax money paid by these Aboriginals is going into a system that disproportionately underfunds their Status Indian brothers and sisters back on reserves where social programs are needed the most. Oh well, maybe Canadians can say a prayer for those reserve Natives the next time they are in church. Incidentally, churches and other religious organizations in Canada don't pay taxes either. But that's an issue for a whole other book.

197

NATIVE GOVERNMENT

"Chief and council or flotsam and jetsam?"

WHEN PEOPLE THINK ABOUT ABORIGINAL GOVERN- ments, they are usually influenced by numerous internet posts, news stories and television programs that paint them as Indian Act slumlords. Just mention "chief and council" and the first word that comes to mind for many Canadians is "corruption." Those with nothing to say usually say it the loudest, and there is no shortage of bellowers who love to educate the masses with their ignorance about Native governance. They love to construct vivid pictures of chiefs lighting cigars with hundred-dollar bills while looking down on their band members and shouting, "Let them eat cake." Meanwhile their constituents are scrounging around in the dirt like truffle hogs. But it's confusing whether this stereotype describes the chief of a reserve or the chief executive officer of a corporation...

It should come as no surprise by now that this stereotype is

blown way out of proportion. The notion that Indian governments are unable to manage their own affairs fits in nicely with
the paternalistic notion that reserves need to be held closely to
the breast of the federal government so it can lead the heathens
toward their "best interests." And what are those best interests?
Say it with me folks: assimilation! This includes the extinguishment of Native rights, the surrender of Indian Land and... well,
you know the drill.

Don't get me wrong, I am not suggesting that all chiefs and
councils are innocent victims of bullying by the mainstream
media. Is it possible that some chief and councils are corrupt? Hell
yeah, they're politicians! That's the nature of the game. However,
the misconception seems to be that *all* Native governments operate under the same levels of deception that you would normally
find on an episode of *Scandal*. In reality, the majority of Native
governments are doing the best they can with the little they get.
Every day they administer funds and manage their bands under
extreme government restrictions against which communities in
mainstream Canada would stage Louis Riel–style rebellions the
likes of which Canada hasn't seen since, well, Louis Riel.

Most Canadians do not understand how the band council system works or how the money supplied to Native communities is
administered. So instead, we are inundated with reports of huge
dollar amounts going to First Nations and screams of "Where did
the money go? In the pockets of the chiefs, that's where!" These
impressions are strange because when I was a kid I lived right
next door to the chief and his house was made of the same Indian
Affairs plywood crap that ours was slapped together with.

Was my chief the exception? If you listen to the pundits they'll
shout "Yes!" and throw around buzz words like "accountability,"
"misspent funds" and "third-party management." They'll compare reserve governments to those in mainstream Canada, even

though this kind of comparison is sort of like comparing bannock and pemmican (translation: they're really different).

Okay, let's roll up our sleeves because there are a lot of issues to address when it comes to the plutocracies that reserves supposedly exist under. The first of which revolves around the notion that Europeans brought civilization, order and civilized government to the primitive, untamed Indians. In the Hollywood westerns the only thing you learn about Native governments is that Indians sit around campfires smoking peace pipes, nodding and saying, "Mmmmm" and "A-ho" a lot. No one's really sure if Natives accomplish anything in these movies, but at least it's more relaxed than Question Period in the House of Commons.

Images like these perpetrate the misconception that Native people were, and continue to be, unable to govern themselves under the sophisticated principles of democracy. This is a real stumbling block when First Nations discuss self-government because many Canadians assume that means going back to living in teepees, smoking the peace pipe and sitting around saying "Mmmmm" and "A-ho." The stereotype also reinforces the notion that Native people are essentially children who must be coddled and remain wards of the state until they move into the twenty-first century, assimilate into Canadian society and, most importantly, give up their land! The reality of historical Native governments is quite the opposite from the stereotype. As we have seen, Native societies operated under such effective governments that the original settlers frequently acquiesced to their Native treaty-making processes.

In the centuries that followed, the strength of tribal governments was severely undermined by the imposition of European governmental practices. This imposition dissolved many fundamentals of Native governance such as equality of tribal members, the division of powers under clans and the ability to assign tribal membership. Before the Indian Act, tribes frequently adopted both Natives and non-Natives who would become equal members of the tribe. Once the Indian Act came into effect, it dictated who could become a member of a tribe based on strict regulations surrounding marriage and blood quantum.

As Native governments were forced into poverty and starvation, they had to enforce these imposed standards of Indian status in order to receive the barest of commodity goods. For tribal members to receive treaty reparations they had to possess "Indian status" as determined by blood quantum (quarter Indian, half Indian, full Indian, etc.). Today, the amount of Indian blood one possesses is still a deciding factor in who can be classified as an Indian in the legal sense.

Even people adopted by Indian tribes, like Johnny Depp by the Comanche Nation or Shania Twain (legally adopted) by her Ojibway stepfather, are unable to claim Indian benefits due to their lack of qualifying percentage of Indian blood. Neither Johnny Depp nor Shania Twain are eligible to receive their five dollars and hunk of government cheese that some treaty tribe members receive each month. Sorry beautiful adopted Indians, you'll have to tighten those purse strings and save up for those items like regular Indians.

Native Funding

Most rights and benefits that a Native person receives are fully regulated by the federal government. Yet many Canadians believe that when the government gives money to Native communities, anyone who can quote a line from *Dances with Wolves* is free to reap the benefits. Like most Native issues, the situation is much more complex than that. The best way to highlight these complexities is to examine the difference between Native and non-Native funding.

In regular-people Canada, there are three levels of government: federal, provincial and municipal. Since each level of government has its own specific responsibilities and corresponding tax regimes, regular-people Canadians receive funding from all three levels of government. For example when Mr. and Mrs. Smith, who live at the end of Cherry Blossom Lane in suburban Canada, go to the doctor that service is funded by the federal and provincial governments. When they send the Smith children to school, that service is funded by the provincial government. When a Smith child brings home a report card that shames the Smith family legacy, they can throw it in the garbage that is picked up by the sanitation department funded by the municipal government. Each of these levels of government has its own administrative body, accounting process, accountability regulations and bureaucrats. Aboriginals living off-reserve are also governed by these three levels of government just like regular-people Canadians. But money that is allotted for on-reserve Aboriginal services primarily goes through one level of government — the federal government. This relationship is supposed to be a continuation of the fiduciary responsibility of the Crown and is regulated by the Department of Aboriginal Affairs and Northern Development (AANDC).

202

AANDC

Before I start in on AANDC, I need to state for the record that my mother used to work for them back when we were still called "Indians" and the department was called "Indian Affairs." That title still makes me giggle because it reminds me of a racially specific sexual activity. (Yes, I am that immature!) So I have a soft spot for Indian Affairs (giggle) but mostly because my mother's paycheques from that department kept me well stocked in Atari video games. (Yes, I am that old!)

From my mother and countless others who have worked for AANDC, I am well aware that the department is faced with a difficult task: administering funds to over 860 reserves and Native communities at differing levels of economic development and governmental assistance. No two Aboriginal communities are the same and administering funds on a per-community basis is no small feat. The department also has no clear-cut agenda like other federal departments. Remember, AANDC is not a Native-run department. Sure, it has some Aboriginal employees and sometimes Native groups lobby to make changes in AANDC policy but for the most part, like the early days of the Indian Department, it is run by an appointed federal minister who directs how things are allowed to work on reserves.

203

Fair enough. In order to ensure responsible government, transparency and fairness, someone has to enforce policy to determine how money is distributed, right? The problem is AANDC, by its own admission, does not have any clear guidelines or policies that determine how money should be distributed to Native communities. Many people assume that funding problems occur at the reserve level, when in fact dysfunction often begins at the federal level before First Nations ever see the money. Before funding can get to Aboriginal communities it must go through AANDC, which distributes the money based on its own "guidelines" and "procedures." A common criticism of AANDC is it has no national standard, such as the equalization program for provinces, for its funding levels. Another problem is that growth rates of funding to First Nations have not been keeping pace with growth rates of funding to the provinces.

In a 2008 report, an Ottawa think tank named the Institute on Governance concluded, "There is a lack of clarity about the overall objectives of the funding arrangements, a lack of coherence among programs and funding authorities that make up the arrangements, and no clear leadership at [AANDC] Headquarters." In her 2011 report, Auditor General Sheila Fraser agreed: "It is often unclear who is accountable to First Nations members for achieving improved outcomes or specific levels of services." Researcher Daniel Wilson has noted that even AANDC officials confirm "there's no system, no standard for calculation. It's not done on a per-capita basis, it's not done on 'What do you have that you currently need to improve?' It's done on a band-by-band basis, seemingly at the whim of administrators in Aboriginal Affairs."

Wow. It's not uncommon for the feds to receive criticism but these are out and out disses! When it comes to keeping pace with needs, the auditor general reported, "The education gap between First Nations living on reserves and the general Canadian population has widened, the shortage of adequate housing on reserves has increased, comparability of child and family services is not ensured." These are major problems, considering the Aboriginal population is increasing at a faster rate than the total population is. Between 1996 and 2006, Statistics Canada found the total Aboriginal population increased forty-five percent compared to an eight-percent increase in the non-Aboriginal population. (I guess those T-Shirts that read *Natives do it better* aren't kidding.) But in the last three budgets the government capped federal spending for Indian and Inuit programs at two percent, half the four-percent annual increase in the Aboriginal population. This two-percent cap also doesn't take inflation into account. Obviously, per capita support is falling behind.

With these funding shortfalls you would think that AANDC, whose job it is to ensure Aboriginals receive adequate funding, would fix its organizational problems and may even tighten its belt. After all, the money that the government budgets for Aboriginal people every year also pays for administration at AANDC. That's right, folks, when the right-wing media screams about the $8 billion that First Nations waste every year, they conveniently forget to mention that a significant portion of Aboriginal funding isn't even getting to Aboriginal communities. Instead it's going to AANDC and outside administrators, lawyers, accountants and other folks who wear ties and charge up billable hours. Given this fact, you'd think AANDC would do everything it could to fix its inefficiencies so more money could get to the Aboriginal communities, right?

Hee hee, let me sing you a song of my people... While the Aboriginal population was growing, funds were capping and money plunging, the number of staff hired at AANDC almost doubled from 3,300 in 1995 to 5,150 in 2010. Salaries plus fees for people like consultants and third-party managers came from money that should have gone to First Nations. In fact, outside consultants, lawyers and accountants receive 1,500 contracts per year from AANDC worth about $125 million (which does not include additional fees First Nations must pay using sources other than AANDC). AANDC claims a large reason for increases in staff is because of the influx of residential school payments as a result of the Truth and Reconciliation hearings. However, reports have revealed that the bulk of these payments have gone into administration and the pockets of shifty lawyers charging exorbitant legal fees and high-interest loans to their impoverished clients waiting for payments.

Okay, so the auditor general, the Assembly of First Nations, most media outlets (not including those who feature Sunshine Girls) and even AANDC agree that the Department of Aboriginal Affairs is a bureaucratic mess with no objectives for funding, no leadership and little to no accountability. Wait a second — I thought that was how First Nations governments were described. When people decry chiefs and councils, they claim the only way to solve reserve problems is through *more* government intervention.

After all, isn't the government supposed to lead us from our heathen ways into the twenty-first century like the Pied Piper? I mean, this is the Great White Father we're talking about here. The chosen one, the one who is supposed to bring balance to the Force and return the ring to Mordor! This is the same federal government that insists Native communities need to pull it together and be more accountable. Funny then that the only policy the government seems to have in place for Aboriginal peoples is the policy of *Do as I say not as I do.*

206   Experts have confirmed what Natives have known all along: that money and services going to reserves is substandard compared to support for regular Canadians. Yet if you ask any number of Canadians, they'll inform you that First Nations not only receive special benefits, they also receive more money than average Canadians. Some right-leaning "thinkers" ignore all mathematical evidence and insist Native communities have way too much money, leading to a sense of entitlement, a lack of work ethic, a welfare state, yada, yada, yada. This must be that "new math" everyone keeps talking about. However, in the real world the math confirms that money going to First Nations is less than the money going to the other Canadians. Let me put it in the form of a mathematical equation: *reserve \$ < regular-folk \$*.

That's pretty easy to understand. The average person on a reserve gets less funding than the average Canadian. This fact should come as a relief to those Canadians who believe Natives don't pay their fair share of taxes (yes, that again) and should therefore not get the same services as regular Canadians. Congratulations, they don't. You win! In addition, the funding that goes to Aboriginals is not regulated by the same policies and procedures as the rest of Canada to ensure funding keeps pace with inflation, population increases, geographical considerations, etc. Despite all this funding kookiness, there are those who persistently insist chiefs are pocketing most of the money and get away with it because there is no accountability on reserves. *That*, they claim, is the real problem. *That* is *not* the real problem.

Native Accountability

Once the federal funding is filtered through AANDC, using who-knows-what process—no seriously, who knows, I'm dying to know—and everyone at the federal level gets their salaries, bonuses, travel expenses and pensions, the leftover money is then washed, inspected for freshness and loaded onto trucks to be taken out to pasture in Aboriginal communities across Canada.

207

The chief and council then distribute the money to departments in their band office to pay for whatever programs are in place. In some band offices you may have Joe who looks after education funding, Mary who looks after agriculture and Bob who looks after health services. In many underfunded communities sometimes Mary has to look after education, agriculture and health services on her own. The federal government does not have any criteria for how these departments are to be run or managed; instead it basically just sends a lump sum to the First Nation and says, "You're on your own." Some might call this a form of self-government; others might call it a form of passing the buck.

Since the chief and council determine how the money will be distributed to the separate departments, this is where the uninformed will jump in and shout, "Yeah, and instead of going to band members or social programs, the chief pockets the cash and goes to Hawaii with his family!" Hold on there Kemo Sabe, you speak with forked tongue! It's actually not that easy to just pocket the cash when you are the chief. There are significant accounting requirements that must be completed every year in order to ensure funding for the next year. We'll get to that in a moment.

First, it's important to note that while people accuse Aboriginal communities of sponging off the government, there are a number of Native communities that are generating "own-source revenue," or as the kids might say, "Handlin' they bin-nuss."

Alternative Funding

Remember, the Indian Act gave the government control over economic and resource development. It also disallowed Natives to engage in economic development on their own land. Only in the last few decades has there been significant change to this arrangement. Since many First Nations have negotiated their own land use agreements, they have been able to form distinct relationships with the federal, provincial and municipal governments. This has created economic opportunities for their communities and many First Nations are now generating revenue from a wide variety of sources.

There are also significant differences in funding for the three Aboriginal groups. Funding for the fifty thousand Inuit in northern communities is mostly covered by four comprehensive land claims settlements that cover forty percent of Canada's land mass. Programs and services are generally provided through territorial or provincial governments as negotiated in their respective land surrenders. Once again, these are arrangements negotiated with the government, which benefits from the surrender of this land. Funding for Metis and non-Status people has always been less cut and dry. However, in January 2013 the federal court ruled that Metis and non-Status Indians fall under federal jurisdiction. Before that ruling, the Metis were often ignored by the federal government, who claimed they were the responsibility of the provinces. Aboriginal Affairs Minister John Duncan appealed the decision (typical!), so it remains to be seen how this one will play out.

208

Despite all the complications surrounding Aboriginal funding, you will still hear people say, "If the chiefs weren't pocketing the money, they could make it stretch further. The rest of Canada makes their social programs work, why can't Indians?" This type of comment is usually followed by the speaker belching, crushing a beer can on his head and wandering away muttering incoherently about the damn RCMP letting them Sikhs wear turbans. But does our imaginary friend have a point? Would Native communities be able to stretch out their limited funding like the rest of Canada if it weren't for all those corrupt billionaire chiefs? Let's ask our old friend the auditor general.

209

Funding Realities

The stated goal of the federal government is to provide a range and level of service to First Nations and Inuit that is comparable to the rest of Canada. However, according to Auditor General Sheila Fraser's 2011 report, the level of service isn't even close; she couldn't conclude the federal government was even concerned with providing the same range and quality of services. So even though First Nations governments are expected to stretch out their money like other Canadian governments, First Nations aren't even close to receiving the same funding or support to stretch. I repeat: *reserve $ < regular-folk $*.

Aboriginal services are funded through "contribution agreements." These agreements are renewed annually, though not always on time as stated in the auditor general's report: "First Nations must often reallocate funds from elsewhere to continue meeting community service requirements." Essentially the report confirms that Native governments are living paycheque to paycheque and when their next cheque is late, as it frequently is, they have to move funds from other programs to pay for immediate needs. I believe the saying is "robbing Peter to pay Paul." So when people scream, "We gave you *x* amount of dollars to pay for agriculture, where did the money go?" a common response might be, "To replace a school that collapsed because it's seventy years old." (For the record, no children were harmed in this imaginary school-collapse scenario.)

In addition to lack of funding, late funding and no clear directives for funding, First Nations face an added burden when it comes to stretching out the funding they get. The costs of living in remote Aboriginal communities are considerably higher than in the rest of Canada. According to the Ontario Association of Food Banks, a bag of apples in Pikangikum averages $7.65 (versus the Canadian average of $2.95) and a loaf of bread in Sandy Lake costs $4.17 (versus the Canadian average of $2.43). Remember Attawapiskat, the community that was constantly asked, "Where did the money go?" A CBC reporter found that in Attawapiskat six apples and four small bottles of juice costs $23.50. So I'm pretty sure that money didn't go to providing the village with an all-you-can-eat buffet.

Unaccountable Corrupt Billionaire Chiefs

There are two myths that continuously dog Aboriginal governments: first, that chief and council are not accountable to the federal government; and second, that chief and council are not accountable to their own people. Historically, the stated intent of the reserve system was to provide First Nations with land to carry on their traditional way of life as self-governing nations, but the reality has proven to be quite the opposite. Even since before Confederation, legislation has ensured that First Nations chiefs and councils would be answerable first and foremost to the cabinet minister responsible for Aboriginal affairs. This is known as a "principal–agent accountability relationship." In this case, the government is the principal and the First Nation is the agent. Under the Indian Act, First Nations are not actually self-governing but rather a type of employee or sub-contractor to AANDC.

In 2006, our old buddy the auditor general reported that the government–First Nations accountability relationship was "unworkable because little legitimacy is attached to it." Another accountability study prepared for AANDC found that, "The emphasis is more on controlling the use of funds than on improving results." Yet another report by the Institute on Governance found that "there are few incentives to perform well, no consequences for poor performance and an absence of performance measures." These findings were applied to both AANDC and the First Nations communities it services.

211

A major problem is that First Nations are at different levels of economic development and experience with government. Limited economic opportunities and resources, coupled with extreme isolation, means that some First Nations require more support. The Institute on Governance further states, "This suggests a highly differentiated approach to accountability to reflect these differences." But what does that word "accountability" really mean? It comes up a lot when referring to Native governments. Many people believe that chiefs and councils do not have to disclose their spending and can run wild like drunken frat boys on spring break, or spend recklessly like drunken sorority girls on Rodeo Drive. As a result, chiefs and councils are frequently labelled "unaccountable."

A recent Ipsos Reid poll asked Canadians whether additional taxpayer money should be withheld from a reserve "until external auditors can be put in place to ensure financial accountability." Eighty-one percent of those asked said "Yes." The poll baffled many First Nations since — are you ready for this? — First Nations already have external auditors to ensure financial accountability! The only thing the poll really uncovered was that neither the pollster nor eighty-one percent of Canadians understand anything about Aboriginal funding.

The contribution agreements that provide First Nations with funding are basically just grants that bands apply for every year. If you have ever worked for an organization that relies on grants to operate, you have basically gone through the same reporting process that First Nations do, except with considerably less paperwork. Anyone who applies for grants on a yearly basis knows you must provide detailed reports of your expenditures in order to get the same amount next year. However, in First Nations communities the lack of available funds is so extreme that the best they can hope for is to get just enough grant money so that the community does not starve before the next reporting period.

Perhaps because the word "Aboriginal" is in AANDC's name, many believe financial information about Native communities is stored in a secret antechamber, locked in a hermetically sealed box and stored next to the remains of a shipwrecked alien. It would be cool if that were the case, but it isn't. National policy states that, "All First Nations, Tribal Councils and Political Organizations that receive transfer payments from any federal government department are required to submit a Schedule of Federal Government Funding." This information is not kept under lock and key, either. Every report that the federal government receives is listed on the AANDC and Health Canada websites for anybody to see. Check it out: you can also see the consolidated budget for the year and even the results from — wait for it — the external auditors!

So when an Ipsos Reid poll asks Canadians if First Nations funds should be withheld unless external auditors are put in place, they might as well be asking, "Should funding for First Nations be withheld until First Nations start using oxygen to breathe?" It already happens! Perpetrating a lie by phrasing it in the form of a question does not make it any less of a lie. Haven't you ever watched *Jeopardy*?

The auditing of First Nations skews even further in favour of the government since the external auditors assigned to First Nations communities are paid by the federal government. This arrangement comes in handy if the government should ever, oh I don't know, maybe want an audit to go a certain way? Now I would never suggest that the federal government might actually target a First Nation through an external audit using dubious criteria and place that community in third-party management to suit the federal government's needs. I would never suggest anything so untoward. Never! Never!!

213

But they do. With ongoing concerns about how First Nations are audited and the methods and standards used, there has been a lot of discussion about creating a First Nations auditor general. This was proposed in 1996 by the Royal Commission on Aboriginal Peoples and was pushed for by the Assembly of First Nations in the Kelowna Accord a decade later. Prime Minister Paul Martin agreed that a First Nations auditor general was required; unfortunately, two months later he lost the 2006 election and the new Conservative government scrapped the Kelowna Accord. Whether or not a First Nations auditor general would provide greater accountability for First Nations governments remains to be seen. One thing the position couldn't possibly do, though, is increase the amount of reporting that AANDC requires of First Nations. Not even Santa Claus has to keep track of as many things as First Nations governments do.

In a 2002 report, the auditor general (yes, her again) estimated that each reserve was required to file 168 annual reports to just the top four federal organizations receiving their reports. The federal government acknowledged the seriousness of the problem and promised action. However, almost ten years later the reporting burden remained the same. But in 2012 AANDC did at least reaffirm what the auditor general had proclaimed a decade earlier: "First Nations and other organizations that receive funding from the Government of Canada are caught in a complex web of reporting requirements, some of which are of dubious usefulness to them or to the organizations seeking the reports."

So the notion that First Nations governments are not accountable to the federal government, external audits or the Canadian taxpayer is — to put it delicately — a load of horse hooey. There still remains the issue of chief and council's accountability to the people they govern. Surprisingly, the most significant problem on reserves is not widespread corruption but rather how a reserve's electoral system works — or doesn't work, as the case may be.

Reserve Elections

Band elections work roughly the same way they do in municipalities or provincial and federal governments. Candidates run for chief and council positions and the regular campaign mudslinging occurs as it does in the rest of Canada. The significant difference is reserve elections happen every two years. Yep, you heard me: two years! Imagine having to elect a new mayor or premier or even a new prime minister every two years. It takes some Canadian politicians two years to decide what they're going to eat for lunch, let alone have to run for re-election.

The short period of time makes it next to impossible to implement policies and see them through, or to establish economic and business relationships. Since the turnover of First Nations governments occurs so frequently, it is difficult for outside businesses or mainstream governments to develop and foster relationships with a chief and council before they have to run for re-election again. It is especially difficult for those who may not have held office before. Once they have learned how to navigate the overwhelming bureaucracies that exist in Native governments, there is another election and the band loses key personnel and has to start all over again. This has created widespread complaints in Native government that with every election they move backwards instead of progressing.

There are some Native communities that have had the same elected officials for numerous election cycles. Many of them remain in power because they are effective leaders, but there are others who have been accused of remaining in power due to a frequently uttered word in Aboriginal communities: *nepotism*. It is not uncommon to hear complaints that some people might have been elected only because they have large families to vote them in. Once these elected officials take power there are further complaints that they only give jobs and benefits to their friends and families. To some extent this does occur, and in smaller communities it is not uncommon to have long histories of competing family bloodlines. So when a chief is elected it usually makes sense to assign positions to family and friends the chief can trust. On reserves this is negatively referred to as "nepotism." In the rest of Canada this is called "politics."

To put the whole nepotism issue into perspective, let's take a look at elections in the rest of Canada. When candidates run for office they require donations for their campaigns. When someone donates to a campaign it is usually because the candidate agrees to fulfill certain promises once elected, ranging from passing a clean-air bill if the supporter is an environmental group or passing a dirty-air bill if the supporter is a resource extraction corporation. Once elected, the candidate is expected to fulfill campaign promises to those who provided the candidate with money or votes.

Frequently, elected officials will reward people from their support bases by securing them advisory positions or jobs as external auditors for First Nations.

Another stereotype about reserve politics is the ease in which elections can be rigged. It's true that voting on-reserve is a little more open to irregularities because whenever an election is held the band appoints an electoral officer to run the election. The electoral officer's job is to prepare the voters list and oversee the election to ensure that everything runs up to snuff. When chiefs are running for re-election, it's possible they could appoint electoral officers who might conveniently forget to put certain names on voters lists or "accidentally lose" some of the ballots. However, there are also protective measures in place to prevent election fraud.

After the close of an election, the candidates can have two representatives monitor the counting of the ballots, or act as their own representative. Electoral officers must then publicly post the results within four days of the election showing the number of votes each candidate received. They must also mail the results to every off-reserve member. So far so good? Even with these measures in place, if someone still wants to contest the legitimacy of the election, there is an appeals process they can file to AANDC. I know what you're thinking: And once the appeal is in the hands of AANDC then you get to see some real federal government ass-kicking transparency, right? Right?

Nope. Ironically, once the appeals process gets to the federal government that's usually where the transparency ends. The appeals process is lengthy and cumbersome as documentation makes its way up the chain of command through AANDC, the assistant deputy minister and then the deputy minister, who decides if an investigation needs to be launched. That investigation then goes back to the regional office of AANDC, which conducts the investigation. Got it?

Okay, remember the stereotype that First Nations governments are not accountable? Well, check this out. During an appeal the regional AANDC gets to decide whom to question, what goes in the report, what facts to gather and what to recommend up the long chain of command back up to the minister. Under the Indian Act there are no rules for this type of investigation in regards to who will receive notice, whether the investigations will be held in public or whether there will be a public hearing—all the things that are supposed to occur in the rest of Canada for an investigation of this nature. In addition, any time an investigation is being conducted, the federal government has the option to place a community under third-party management completely at its whim. This is not an option at any other level of government in Canada.

217

This brings me back to the conflict of interest over the federal government's fiduciary responsibility to First Nations versus their ability to benefit from First Nations, which also applies to elections. Let's say a band member appeals an election but the chief and council in question are known to be "co-operative" to the federal government in areas such as land surrender or resource extraction or taxation policies. Since the investigation is being conducted by the federal government, it can guide it any way it wants to protect a co-operative chief and council. There is nothing anyone can do about it either, because the federal government gets to pick and choose what information is investigated. On the other hand, if a chief is known to be "uncooperative," like demanding housing, treaty reparations, past due funds, etc., the investigation could sway very unfavourably for that chief and nobody would ever know what criteria the unfavourable review was based on. Now, I would never suggest the federal government would ever do this. I would never suggest they would ever do anything so untoward. Never! Never!

But they do. In addition to the appeals process lacking

transparency, it can often take as long as twelve to eighteen months before a decision is rendered. That's twelve to eighteen months of a twenty-four-month term in office, which means by the time a decision is made on the legitimacy of a chief and council, their term will have almost been done. The reality is, First Nations are overly accountable to the federal government but the federal government does not have to be accountable to First Nations. So with practically every aspect of First Nations government under scrutiny, why do accusations of corruption persist?

Chief and Council Accountability

In Canada today there seems to be two types of First Nations economies: those with extreme poverty and those with comparative wealth. The most common is the extreme poverty variety. In some of these communities the unemployment rate can be as high as ninety-five percent so being on chief and council is an attractive proposition. Political leadership guarantees you an income and control over all resources and funding in your community. In some of the more economically advanced communities, the chief and council might be in charge of million-dollar budgets and large corporate holdings. In all cases, the race for chief and council can get downright ugly. In many communities the chief and council are the only ones with any real economic opportunities. For those left on the outside, it can feel like they are the "have-nots" while the chief and councils are the "haves." The "have-nots" often feel powerless and view the chief and council as corrupt plutocracies that are ignoring the people. But are they right? Are the chief and council really that unaccountable to their people?

The Indian Act's emphasis on the power and authority of the minister has a major impact on the quality of democracy in First Nations governments. Every section of the Act that sets out a reserve's decision-making ability also allows the minister to override decisions made by chief and council. Ministerial power and authority over all band governance is largely responsible for the lack of autonomy and responsibility to the community. Many Native leaders have complained that their leadership under the Indian Act is largely to administer Indian Affairs money. Rather than being a political leader, this relationship makes chief and council another bureaucrat of the system or another employee of AANDC. Since virtually all authority and funds come directly through AANDC, their mandate to govern comes directly from AANDC as well. However, there is one thing that chief and council do have full authority over — their salaries!

When both First Nations politicians *and* other Canadian politicians have the ability to set their own income levels, why is it considered such a sin that the Native leaders do it? Could it be that many Canadians believe that First Nations leaders are morally incapable of paying themselves a reasonable wage? Read any website comments on Native accountability and this appears to be the pervasive view of Native leaders. Perhaps a reason for this distrust is that until recently, chiefs and councils had to publicly disclose how their budgets were spent with the exception of their salaries. An outside observer might assume that since chiefs do not have to *publicly* disclose their salaries, then they can give themselves multi-million dollars in income and nobody would be any the wiser. Well, you know the old saying about making assumptions: "It makes you look like a douchebag" (or something like that).

Given what we know about Native reporting practices, let's examine this scenario logically. The key word in the hullabaloo surrounding Native accountability is chief and councils do not have to "publicly" disclose their income. This is an important point to make and there is a reason for it. Canada's Privacy Act, which applies to all Canadians, limits the government's ability to disclose personal information. The Indian Act establishes that First Nations income earned on-reserve is considered personal property even if that income derives from public funds such as federal funding. In regular-people Canada, politicians also receive their income from public funds but because they earn their money off-reserve their income is not considered private property. Therefore it is not protected under Canada's Privacy Act like First Nations income. With me so far?

220

Previous court rulings affirmed that First Nations income is considered private property, so allowing the government to force someone to reveal the amount of their private property was unconstitutional. This didn't mean that First Nations leaders couldn't voluntarily disclose their income. In December of 2010, the Assembly of First Nations passed a resolution agreeing to publish its salaries and expenses and pushed for a non-binding resolution for First Nations governments to become more accountable. In addition, a loophole in the Privacy Act states that governments can disclose personal information if another law requires it. So in March 2013 the federal government enacted Bill C-27, the First Nations Financial Transparency Act, to become the other law that overrides the Privacy Act and requires First Nations to disclose personal information.

Pretty sneaky, huh? What's even sneakier is how the federal government convinced the Canadian people that Native governments were all oozing with widespread corruption because they didn't have to publicly disclose their income, but now that Bill C-27 was in town it was going to wipe out corruption like the second coming of Eliot Ness and his Untouchables. This whole situation was strange considering that First Nations audits, public accounts, salaries, honorariums and expenses were already reported to the federal government. If auditors found any irregularities or evidence of corruption, they could easily launch an investigation or place the First Nation under third-party management. If band governments tried to hide money from their reports then any money not accounted for, including salaries and expenses, could result in audits and delays in funding for the next year. The whole issue made very little sense, unless you consider the source of the controversy.

Bill C-27: The First Nations Financial Transparency Act

In 2010, the Canadian Taxpayers Federation (CTF), an "independent" think tank, published documents alleging that some First Nation chiefs earned more than the prime minister of Canada. The findings were met with criticism that the report was full of inaccurate data. The Assembly of First Nations claimed the watchdog organization inflated the salary numbers by including travel expenses and other costs that, in some cases, increased the numbers by thirty percent. Regardless, the incident gave birth to the First Nations Financial Transparency Act, which required that chiefs make their salaries, expenses and other such stuff public. The Act brought cheers from the legions of uninformed who believed Aboriginals were finally going to have to disclose their financial information and stop being so gosh-darn corrupt.

The CTF, along with another "independent" think tank—the Frontier Centre for Public Policy—reported that from 2008–09, Chief Glenn Hudson of Peguis First Nation earned more than $200,000. A further 2010 report by the CTF suggested there were at least thirty band chiefs in Canada who were paid more than the average premier. They also profiled Chief Roger Redman, who made an after-tax income of $194,737 for leading a band of only 443 people. They pointed out that Redman earned more than the prime minister of Canada, who led a country of thirty-five million. As stated before, it's hard to know the accuracy of these figures because there is controversy surrounding the CTF's accounting. Incidentally, if you are an anti-Aboriginal special interest group, I cannot think of a more perfect chief to target than one with the last name *Redman*.

It's important to note that groups like the Canadian Taxpayers Federation and the Frontier Centre for Public Policy are well-known right-wing organizations who push for less taxation and less government interference for regular Canadians. However when it comes to First Nations they tend to push for more government interference. As we have seen, more government interference usually means dissolving tribal autonomy and sovereign rights, which is very much in line with the desired goal of conservative interests. Since these so-called "independent" think tanks are funded by right-wing corporations, the philosophies and goals of their corporate funders frequently make their way into their "independent" reports. The CTF is a major supporter of the oil and gas sector, which has vested interests in resource extraction on Indian-held land.

So now, theoretically, truth and justice can rain down upon the corrupt chiefs and politicians. But how much will Bill C-27 actually change? First Nations are already audited and AANDC already has the power to take over First Nations finances and impose a third-party manager. The only change is really making sure that chiefs' and councils' expenses and salaries are placed on a website to be more easily accessed by band members or other Canadians. Fine, fair enough. However, there is still the issue that any First Nations who do not comply with the posting of their salaries and expenses can have their funding withheld. This move is unprecedented, with First Nations the only grant recipients at any level of the Canadian government that has had this imposed on them. Hmmm... I thought right-wing special interest groups were opposed to race-based policy? It's a two-way street, kiddies — make up your mind.

By the way, Bill C-27 does not apply to the twenty-three or so First Nations operating under self-government agreements or to the Inuit. Aboriginals operating under self-governments establish their own internal governance systems and oversee economic development, health, education and social services. Not a bad deal. Unfortunately, AANDC says that on average it takes about fifteen years to negotiate a final self-government agreement. For those who still rely on AANDC funding, the federal government is once again imposing paternalistic regulations on First Nations that allow for greater power to extinguish First Nations autonomy.

Look, we live in an imperfect world, and when all is said and done there is going to be a small percentage of chiefs and councillors who insist on paying themselves more than ministers and prime ministers. I think we can all agree that they suck. However, let me remind you one more time that regular Canadian politicians not only earn a salary, but they also earn generous pensions and are often guaranteed lucrative positions in the private sector, or on boards of directors or advisory councils, when they are done with politics. Not so with First Nations. The only thing they're really eligible for is third-party management. Which brings me to my final topic! (I really gotta work on my segues.)

Third-party Management

If First Nations do not comply with federal reporting practices based on criteria known only to the federal government, they can be placed under third-party management. This means that if the government does not believe a band can manage its own affairs, then the federal government can assign an outside management company to take over the band's administration. As we saw during the Attawapiskat crisis, the government didn't hesitate to place that community under third-party management; but if the government used the same criteria for the rest of the country, much of Canada would be under third-party management by now.

For example, the City of Toronto ran a deficit for years as the federal, provincial and municipal governments spent a combined total of $24,000 a year on each Torontonian. Attawapiskat, which is funded almost solely by the federal government, received only about $11,355 per capita to supply programs and infrastructure to its 1,550 residents. And that's way more than the average on-reserve Native receives! Hey Toronto, here's an annoying phrase us Natives get all the time: "Where did all the money go? In the pockets of your crooked leaders, that's where!" Doesn't feel very good, does it?

A recent publicly disclosed example of third-party-manager fees were those paid for Barriere Lake. When the community took political action on some of its outstanding issues, Canada suddenly decided that the community needed to be put under third-party management. What a coincidence. According to AANDC, the outside accounting firm was paid $600,000 a year with money that was supposed to go to First Nations social programs. So the next time someone screams, "Hey Indians, were did the money go?" the answer should be, "To pay for some rich white guy's private jet!"

Almost every time a First Nation goes into third-party management, it comes out with as much debt as it had going in — or more. This means the government pays big-shot accountants over half a million dollars a year, as in Barriere Lake, to sort out a community's finances and not even these geniuses can use their financial super powers to get the community into the black. This is a pretty good indication that the problem is not always fiscal mismanagement, but rather insufficient resources to deliver the programs needed. Still, the federal government and right-wing media continue to scream, "Where did the money go?" Come to think of it, as a taxpaying Canadian I could easily scream the same thing at the federal government every single day. But I'm sure they would have solid answers and carefully prepared financial records. I mean, they're not First Nation governments so they must be one hundred percent accountable, right? Right?

Nope. In what can only be described as a hysterical burst of karma, just a few short months after the government and media screamed, "Where did the money go?" at Attawapiskat, the auditor general released a report that found the federal government could not account for over $3 billion in anti-terrorism initiatives. Furthermore, it had no idea whether or not it had met any of its objectives in keeping terrorists out of Canada and deterring attacks. This revelation must have been especially frightening for Canadians considering that when First Nations gather to protest, the government and media often refer to them as "terrorists."

So when the rest of Canada finally turned around and screamed "Where did the money go?" at the federal government, the Conservatives just shrugged and in their best Brooklyn accent responded, "Fuhgetaboutit." I would bet dollars to Tim Hortons doughnuts that if a First Nation couldn't account for even *three thousand* dollars, groups like the CTF would be screaming bloody murder and lobbying for third-party management faster than you can say "First Nations transparency."

But the hypocrisy does not end there. When it comes to handling their own finances, Canada and its provinces are prime candidates for third-party management. Canada's federal deficit was projected in early 2014 to be $16.6 billion. This number does not include the $3.1 billion terrorism funds that are unaccounted for since that money is not really gone — they just don't know where it is. Fuhgetaboutit. Canada's provinces have been in debt for years, some of them decades. Quebec is the winner when it comes to candidacy for third-party management with more than $21,000 owed for every man, woman and child. For the fiscal year 2012–2013, Ontario ran a $9.2-billion deficit. Even oil-rich Alberta ran a $2.8-billion deficit for the 2012–2013 fiscal year. Yes, you read those provincial deficit amounts correctly: billions! Third-party management anyone? Anyone?

The criteria for placing a First Nation in third-party management is probably one of the most hypocritical of all the federal government's policies. If it had to apply the same rules to its own governments, I guarantee the words "transparency," "accountability" and "third-party management" would not be bandied about as freely as they are. So for the small percentage of Indian reserves that actually do suffer from corruption, they have the federal government to thank for that. Reserve governments are basically just extensions of the bureaucracies of the larger federal government. So if your reserve is extremely good at being corrupt, you can take pride in knowing that it learned from the best.

THE FUTURE

"Indianfinity and beyond!"

So, what does the future hold for my high-cheekboned, hairless, mostly taxpaying people? More importantly, why should North America be paying attention? The simple answer is this: North America has some serious debts they need to settle with Native people before they can truly consider themselves a free country and/or true democracy. As more court cases rule in favour of Native land claims, the Canadian public is being forced to reassess its relationship with First Nations. As more Aboriginals learn the truth about Canada's history and, in turn, educate non-Native Canadians, political leaders are being forced to admit that they have "a lot of 'splaining to do." As more Aboriginals take to the airwaves, internet and social media sites, they are slowly guaranteeing that the Canadian public is no longer able to ignore the century's worth of shady dealings they have endured from first contact to present day.

The policies of assimilation that were forced on Aboriginal people over the centuries do not appear to have achieved their desired goals. While it's true that the majority of First Nations are leaving their reserves and entrenching themselves in the dominant culture, most of them are building new communities of Native solidarity and resistance in urban centres. More than ever, Aboriginals are achieving the highest levels of education and their influence is being felt in all levels of government. Despite the government's desired goal of utilizing education to assimilate all Aboriginal people, Aboriginal people are actually utilizing that education to strengthen their resistance against colonization. Boy did that policy ever backfire!

Even through the internet, Aboriginal people are sharing strategies and interacting with fellow indigenous people, not only across the continent but around the world. Movements like Idle No More have been extremely jarring to those who once believed that Native people were unable to organize, unable to articulate their struggle and unable to garner support from outside the Native community. What has been even more jarring is how widespread that support has been for the Native cause from every corner of the globe.

The struggles, deceptions and misconceptions that face Aboriginal peoples today are no longer just Native issues. With so much of the world's power and wealth being held by one percent of the population and human rights violations being perpetrated so freely and frequently across the globe, it is becoming much easier for the average person to empathize and relate to the oppression that Native people have endured for centuries. As Native people take to social media as well as the mainstream media, the world is now opening its eyes to the extent of the struggles facing Native North Americans in a continent where such struggles were once considered unfathomable. And you know what? The general public isn't willing to turn a blind eye anymore.

However, for those who stand to benefit from the disappearance of Aboriginal peoples, the accessibility of the internet and other media has also led to a greater influx of lies, stereotypes and misinformation about Native people across a much wider platform. That's right, this isn't your grandfather's racism anymore. This racism is high-tech and in high def.

No worries, though. Native people are angry but they're not dissuaded and they sure as hell aren't defeated. Native people were never a vanishing race and they're not going away now. Not since first contact have Native people been so active, so prepared and so ready to change perceptions in order to reclaim our past glory and the inevitable glory of our future. As Native people achieve higher levels of education, they are becoming increasingly more adept at speaking the so-called "white-man's language." And Native people are speaking it loudly and without restraint. This is one of the most powerful tools we Natives have at our disposal right now, because we are able to use this language to hold our governments accountable for their past and present obligations, and we're able to do it using their words. If there is one thing that Native people excel at, it is utilizing the power of words and language. Hey, we come from an oral tradition remember? Or as the west coast Indians might say, "The squeaky wheel gets the oolichan grease." So in answer to the question, "What does the future hold for Aboriginal people?" the future holds noise. Lots and lots of noise.

A Note on Sources

IT MAY SURPRISE YOU TO HEAR THIS, ESPECIALLY IF you've just finished reading this book, but I am not a historian, legal scholar, doctor or priest. If I have succeeded in making you believe otherwise, it's all thanks to the magic of research. *Peace Pipe Dreams* is meant to be a quick and dirty introduction to the truth behind the stereotypes, and one of its central messages is, *Don't believe everything you read about Indians.* But if you're eager for more fun facts to impress people at dinner parties, there are a few trustworthy sources out there, if you know where to look. Follow me as I take you on an enchanted journey through the world of my research methods.

To find all the cold, hard, occasionally depressing facts about Native people in Canada, look no further than our old friend, the Canadian government. The website for Aboriginal Affairs and Northern Development Canada (previously known by the amusing name of "Indian Affairs") has lots of information about the on-again off-again relationship between the government and Aboriginal communities. This includes information about historical treaties, Indian status and legal benefits, government initiatives and funding—all that good stuff. I've also spent some quality time perusing the figures on the Statistics Canada website, where I got my facts about Aboriginal health, demographics, employment and crime, among other things. If you're looking for a good beach read, I would also recommend the Indian Act and the Constitution Acts, which are available on the Canadian government's Justice Laws website: http://laws-lois.justice.gc.ca.

231

For anyone who still needs convincing that Native people aren't stuck in the past, just take a look at all the fantastic First Nations resources available on the web. A few of the websites I used the most were Our Voices (http://www.aboriginalgba.ca), devoted to the study of Aboriginal women's health, the Aboriginal Healing Foundation (http://www.ahf.ca), committed to supporting the survivors of residential schools, Native Languages of the Americas (http://www.native-languages.org), preserving the use of Native American languages, and Seven Circles Foundation (http://www.sevencircles.org), promoting the continued practice of traditional spiritual ceremonies.

To keep up with all the late breaking news in Indian country, I also consulted some news sources. I'm contractually obligated to mention that I rely on CBC News for many of my Canadian journalism needs (by the way, have I mentioned that past episodes of *Revision Quest* are available on the CBC website?). I also found several useful articles on *First Nations Drum*, Canada's largest First Nations newspaper.

And just so you don't think I ain't no good at no book learning, I should also mention that I also referred to a few academic sources in the course of my research. A couple of the articles that were most helpful are "Native Americans, Neurofeedback, and Substance Abuse Theory" by Matthew J. Kelley, which discusses factors behind Native alcohol abuse; "Aboriginal Mental Health: The Statistical Reality" by Saman Khan; and "Gender, Race, and the Regulation of Native Identity in Canada and the United States: An Overview" by Bonita Lawrence, which is about gender discrimination in official definitions of who gets to be called an Indian.

There are many other great sources out there that I don't have room to mention here, so take this list as a starting point to go forth and conquer Native stereotypes on your own. I think you'll find the power was in you this whole time.

Index

A

Aboriginal, term, 12, 17–18, 28

Aboriginal Affairs and Northern
Development Canada
(AANDC), 17. *See also* Indian
and Northern Affairs Canada
(INAC)
and First Nations government,
216, 217, 219, 222–23
and funding, 202–5, 211–14
and social assistance, 183–86

Aboriginal Healing Foundation, 123

Alaskan Native, term, 20–21

alcohol and First Nations
alcoholism, 85, 87, 93, 122, 127
binge drinking, 91, 100, 101, 102,
108
deaths and injuries, alcohol-
related, 100–101, 103, 106–7

genetic factors, misconception
about, 85–86, 87, 94–98, 101,
109
history, 87–94
and mental health, 98, 103–6
temperance and prohibition, 85,
93
treatment programs, 108

Algonquian, people, 21, 26, 28, 146

American Indian, term, 8, 20, 22, 28

American Indian Religious
Freedom Act, 1978 (AIRFA),
130

American Revolutionary War, 52,
55–56, 148

Amerind, term, 23, 28

Anishinaabe, people. *See* Ojibway
(Anishinaabe), people

Arapaho, people, 51

Arawak, people, 35

Assembly of First Nations, 158, 196, 213, 221

assimilation attempts, 65, 83, 116, 125, 153, 179, 199, 228

Attawapiskat crisis, 210, 224, 225

Avatar, 42–43

B

Beothuk, people (historical), 24

British North America Act. *See* Constitution Act of 1867 (British North America Act)

C

Caddo Nation, 119

Canadian-American Reciprocity Treaty, 138

Canadian Charter of Rights and Freedoms, 155, 166

Canadian constitution, 12, 17, 163, 180. *See also* Constitution Act of 1867 (British North America Act); Constitution Act of 1982

ceremonial pipes, 131–32

Cherokee, people, 60, 78

Cheyenne, people, 51, 116

Columbus, Christopher, 13–16, 35–36, 42

Comanche Nation, 201

Constitution Act of 1867 (British North America Act), 17, 150, 165–69

Constitution Act of 1982, 17, 52, 148

Covenant Chain, 142–43

Cree, people, 152, 155, 158

cultural appropriation, 76–77, 83

Custer, George Armstrong (General), 51, 129–30

D

Dakota Sioux, people, 49, 119

Dances with Wolves, 31, 45, 201

Denning, Alfred (Lord Denning), 156

E

enfranchisement, 169, 174, 177, 179. *See also* Gradual Civilization Act; Gradual Enfranchisement Act

Eskimo, term, 21. *See also* Inuit

F

First Nations, term, 8, 12, 18, 28

First Nations Financial Transparency Act, 221

First Nations government, 198–200. *See also* self-government accountability, 207–8, 211–13, 218–23 elections, 214–17

funding, 201–6, 209–10

pre-contact, 26–27, 41, 61

and third-party management, 224–26

First Nations medicine, 36–37, 39–41

First Nations religions, 112–15, 136

prohibitions, 32, 64, 129, 174, 175–76, 179

First Nations tax exemptions, 187–90

income tax, 193–97

sales tax, 191–92

Fox, people, 49

Fraser, Sheila, 209, 211, 213, 225

French and Indian Wars, 61. *See also* Seven Years' War

G

Ghost Dance, 118, 119, 129, 130

Gradual Civilization Act, 120, 169, 174

Gradual Enfranchisement Act, 120, 169

Gwich'in, people, 157–58

Gwich'in Comprehensive Land Claim Agreement, 157

H

Haida, people, 60

Hudson's Bay Company, The, 48, 49–50, 150, 151

Huron, people, 49, 144, 146

I

Idle No More, 45, 228

Indian, term, 8, 9, 13–16, 18, 28

Indian Act, 16–17, 153–54, 169, 172, 180, 181

and First Nations government, 211, 217, 218, 219, 220

improvements to, 178–79

repressive measures of, 119, 151, 156, 170, 173–78, 201, 208

and taxes, 188–89, 195

Indian agents, 64–65, 125, 170, 172, 173, 176, 177, 181

Indian and Northern Affairs Canada (INAC), 119, 151, 167, 169, 172, 176. *See also* Aboriginal Affairs and Northern Development Canada (AANDC)

Indian Department, 124, 146, 148, 173, 203

Indian Intercourse Acts, 51

Indian princess, term, 26–27

Indian Religious Crimes Code, 129. *See also* First Nations religions: prohibitions

Indian Reorganization Act, 181

235

Indian Status, 10, 125, 144, 169, 201
and taxes, 188–93, 197
and women, 170, 179
Indian Wars, 27, 119, 130
indigenous, term, 22–23, 28
Inherent Right to Self-Government Policy, 158
Inuit
people, 12, 18, 21, 64, 88, 95, 96, 101–2, 103–4, 155, 158, 182, 189, 208
term, 21
See also Nunavut Land Claims Agreement
Iroquois, people, 60, 66, 142–44, 146

J
James Bay and Northern Quebec Agreement, 155
Jay Treaty, 10–12, 138

K
Kelowna Accord, 213

L
Lakota Sioux, people, 119, 129
land claims, 156–57, 160, 166, 168, 171, 176, 208
Last of the Mohicans, The (book), 57

Last of the Mohicans, The (film), 45
Little Big Horn, Battle of, 51, 129–30

M
Maliseet, people, 144
Massachusetts, people, 26
media portrayals of First Nations
adoption stories, 42–43
advertising, 65–66
captivity narratives, 58–63
comics, 74–75
romanticizing and demonizing, 32–34, 43–45
westerns, 25, 44–45, 63, 200
Meech Lake Accord, 156
Mesoamerican civilizations, 39
Metacomet, 27, 54–55, 56
Metis
people, 12, 18, 101, 148, 153, 155, 182, 189–90
term, 12, 18
See also Sahtu Dene and Metis Comprehensive Land Claim Agreement, 157
Mi'kmaq, people, 144–45
Mohawk of Kanesatake, people, 157

N
Narragansett, people, 28

Index

Native American, term, 8, 21–22, 28

Native American Church, 133

Native American Graves Protection and Repatriation Act (NAGPRA), 131

Nazis, 68–69, 120

Nisga'a, people, 154

North American Free Trade Agreement (NAFTA), 138, 158, 181

Numbered Treaties, 152–53, 157, 159, 171

Nunavut Land Claims Agreement, 157

O

Odawa, people, 49

Office of Native Claims, 154

Ojibway/Anishinaabe, people, 19, 20, 49, 201

Oka Crisis, 45, 157

Oliver Act, 175

P

Pan-Indianism, 19, 38, 64, 66, 112

papoose, term, 28

Peace and Friendship Treaties, 145, 180

peace pipes. *See* ceremonial pipes

Peguis First Nation, 221

peyote, 118, 130, 132–33

Potawatomi, people, 49

Q

Quebec, 69

R

"Red Paper," 23

Red Sucker Lake First Nation, 156

redskin/red Indian, term, 23–24, 25

repatriation of artifacts and remains, 130–31. *See also* Native American Graves Protection and Repatriation Act (NAGPRA)

reserves, 153, 171–72, 173, 175, 177, 178, 180, 182, 210, 228

and housing, 184–87

and taxes, 189–97

residential schools, 65, 119–22, 174

legacy of, 122–28

Royal Commission on Aboriginal Peoples, 157, 163, 213

Royal Proclamation of 1763, 50–52, 146–47, 148, 151, 163, 165–67, 169, 171

S

Sahtu Dene, people, 158

Sahtu Dene and Metis Comprehensive Land Claim Agreement, 157

Sauk, people, 49

savage, term, 25

Scott, Duncan Campbell, 65, 124

self-government, 200, 207, 210, 211, 223

Seneca, people, 118

Seven Years' War, 50, 52, 145, 146

Shubenacadie Nation, 145

Shuswap (Secwepemc), people, 19, 78

Sioux, people, 51

sports mascots, 30, 69–74. *See also* Washington Redskins

squaw, term, 25–26

Status. *See* Indian Status

stereotypes about First Nations
alcoholism, 85–87, 105, 109. *See also* alcohol and First Nations
appearance, 30, 58, 77–80, 82
corruption, 198–99, 216–17. *See also* First Nations government: accountability
"noble savage," 34, 43, 53, 55, 57, 65, 66, 69, 70, 176
pre-contact society, 38. *See also* First Nations government: pre-contact
religion, 112, 131–32, 136. *See also* First Nations religions
taxes and benefits, 102, 140, 182–84 187, 195–96. *See also* First Nations tax exemptions; reserves: and housing; treaties

"vanishing Indian," 44, 66, 75, 116, 177–78, 229
See also media portrayals of First Nations

Sun Dance ceremony, 116, 130, 134

Supreme Court of Canada, 145, 154, 162, 163, 168, 180, 189

sweat lodges, 112, 133–34

T

taxes. *See* First Nations tax exemptions

traditional names of First Nations, 18–19, 28

treaties, 138–41, 142–64, 165, 167, 173, 180, 192. *See also individual treaty names*

Treaty of Paris, 138, 149

Treaty of Utrecht, 144

Trudeau, Pierre, 154, 155

Truth and Reconciliation Commission, 121, 205

Two Row Wampum Treaty, 142

U

Umbrella Final Agreement, 157

Upper Canada Treaties, 148

V

Vancouver Island Treaties, 148

vision quests, 134, 136